Saint Fred

...the last Latin teacher

By Steve Buttress

Other works by Steve Buttress:

The Next American Hero Series:

> Book One: Standing Too Close to the Flame

> Book Two: Talks with Crows

> Book Three: ReBecoming (mid-2011)

Knowing Kearney...Uncovering the Secrets of Kearney's Success

Chief Many Blankets O'Brien...the Irish, the Pawnee and the Mormons on the Platte

Merry Crittermas . . . a children's Christmas story

Merry Crittermas II . . . the world learns the 'true' story of Christmas

Merry Crittermas III . . . continuing adventures in Critterland

Dedicated to Fred and Margaret,

happy survivors

"The reasonable man adapts himself to the world. The unreasonable one persists in trying to adapt the world to himself. Therefore all progress depends on the unreasonable man."

George Bernard Shaw

The Cast of Characters

Fred...self-appointed saint and hero of the piece
Amelia, aka Fluffy...his oldest sister
Margaret...his sister
Albert...brother
Victor...brother
Carl, aka Poopdeck Pappy...brother
Joe...brother
Steve...nephew
Mary...step-daughter
Julie...niece
Michael...nephew
JB...nephew
Mark...nephew

This is as close as I can get it. The old voices are all still now. They told stories which are now darting around my memory. They left scatterings of paper. I've filled in the gaps with my best guess of how it might have happened. Or maybe my hope for how it did. Or maybe with a novelist's prerogative of improving the truth.

<u>Margaret</u>

They say that adults can't truly remember events that occurred early in life, before the age of six, say. They say that the things you remember are stories you've heard about those early years, not the event themselves. I read that somewhere, some psychologist from a university back east. The gist of the article was that children's brains have not developed that type of memory capacity at those early ages. The researcher meant well. He was encouraging parents and siblings, other relatives too I suppose, to tell growing children stories of their early years so that the events won't be lost. That would be a good thing. But he was wrong. He should have talked to me before he wrote that article. I remember things from way before I was six.

I remember our home at 611 Castle Street. I remember the small confectionary that fronted on Castle, and the one-step wooden stoop at the entrance. I remember sitting on that stoop with my brothers Joe and Freddie, soaking up the sun and watching Mama grill the wieners which she wrapped in a napkin and sold to folks walking past. I remember the sizzling sound of them cooking, and the spicy aroma that they gave off. Those are memories of being there, not of somebody later telling me about it. The sound, the smell, the jostling with my brothers.....those are things I remember.

I remember a low oak counter just to the right as you entered the store, and a glass-covered case where the candies were displayed. Papa always made sure that glass was wiped clean every day. It was part of the ritual of opening the store. "Cleana da glass," he'd say as he applied a clean rag and elbow grease to the task. I remember the two stairs at the rear of the store, and the solid wooden door that separated the store from our home. I remember the intricate flower pattern in the door handle. They don't seem to make door knobs that

1

fancy anymore. Cheaper probably, but not as memorable. I remember the long hallway that stretched out before you as that door swung open. Mama and Papa's room was first, then the room I shared with my big sister Amelia, then the boys' room. The room at the back end of the hallway was always saved for boarders. I think Papa needed the little extra money that would bring in.

Sometimes it was used for relatives who had just arrived from "the old country," as Papa would call it. I remember for sure that Uncle Tommie stayed there for a while. I know that it was my memory, not a story somebody told me. Nobody could have told me, because nobody else knew this part. It was late in 1916, a few months before Freddie was born. On Christmas Eve, we we're all sitting around the table, Uncle Tommie next to me, when Mama served us spaghetti. It was in a large china bowl that had little red roosters decorating the rim, and she had it resting on a thick towel draped across her huge stomach, inside of which was the soon-to-be-born Fred. Uncle Tommie started laughing uncontrollably. When he finally could catch his breath he said, well, he said it in Italian, which I didn't understand, but then Papa started laughing the same way, and when he could talk he told us what Uncle Tommie had said. "That'sa mighty fine serving tray you got there, Rosa." Then we all laughed too, except Mama. She tried to scowl. Perspiration was running down her forehead and onto her cheeks. I could tell she was tired. I think maybe there was a hint of a smile which put the lie to the feigned indignation.

The funny line wasn't the part that can prove my early memory. Someone could have told me that part. Everyone at the table heard it, and it became a fixture in our family history. No Christmas dinner after that was complete until someone turned to Mama and said, "That'sa fine serving tray you got there, Rosa." It always got that rollicking Stefano laugh. That part just helps me date it, December 24, 1916.

The part that proves that I can remember something from that night, a secret that nobody else could have told me, was this. After Mama and Papa had tucked me into bed and before Amelia had come in,

Uncle Tommie came into the room. He sat on the bed next to me. He told me that I was as beautiful as my father had said in a letter he had written Tommie. Then Uncle Tommie reached into his coat pocket and pulled out a piece of paper-wrapped candy.

"I got this at the docks in Napoli. I didn't have enough money to buy candy for all the children. Just enough for one, for you, the baby in the family for another few weeks. Then a new baby will come along, and you'll be a big girl." He said it all in his broken English, with every other word an Italian one. I didn't have any trouble understanding this mix of languages. It was the standard brew in our home, an immigrant family gradually weaving its way into a new culture.

I loved being the baby, my father's favorite I was sure. I loved Uncle Tommie for telling me I was beautiful, and for telling me that my father thought I was beautiful too. And I loved the secret piece of candy. I hid it in my sock drawer and didn't eat it for a long time. After I ate it I saved the paper wrapper, stuck into the pages of my Sunday missal, because it reminded me of such a happy time. So there's a memory, certified and guaranteed, from when I was four years and four months old.

I remember December 25, 1917 too. I was in Columbus, Ohio. Grandma had come to Wilmington to get me. Papa had been sick that year, 1917. He couldn't work anymore. He was in and out of the hospital all year long. I know things were tough for our family that year. Grandma told me so. There was no income and all the doctor and hospital expenses. That's why Grandma came and took me back to Columbus with her. To help out Mama.

I think that sometimes Papa was acting 'out of his head' was the way Grandma said it. I never saw it, but I heard that he got violent at times. It was the disease that did it. Papa was a very gentle man. He would never be violent on his own.

I remember the last time I saw Papa. It was in the hospital, just before Grandma took me north. He was covered up with white sheets, all the

3

way up to his chin. The shade was drawn on the window so it was dark in the room. I remember the smell of the room, a bitter sort of chemical odor. There was a light on the stand beside his bed, and I could see his face by the yellow light from the lamp. I remember being scared. He didn't look right. He heard us come in and he slowly opened his eyes and turned his face toward me. He could tell I was anxious. He was too weak to lift me up, so he asked the nurse standing next to Grandma to lift me up on the bed next to him.

"Come close, Little Princess," he whispered. I think it was all the voice he had left in him. He pushed the sheet down to free his arms, then he pulled me to his chest. If I remember one thing in my whole life, it was the feeling of that hug, that last hug. It was warm, and it was strong, and it made me believe, at least for then, what he said next.

"Thing'sa gonna be just fine. You'll see. You live in a strong family."

It was a few weeks later, Christmas day, that a neighbor knocked on Grandma's door. It was the barber who had come over from Casal, the same village as Grandma and Grandpa. He lived down the street, and he was the only one in our neighborhood who had a telephone. Grandma said that he had 'done very well for a Tedeschi.' I got the feeling, probably from the way she said 'Tedeschi,' that maybe Grandma didn't like him very much. I know she didn't like the news he carried, but I also think she wasn't surprised. She thanked Mr. Tedeschi for braving the storm outside and offered him a cup of coffee before he went back out. I remember he said 'no' and left as quickly as he had arrived. Then Grandma turned to me, walked me over to a huge overstuffed chair, sat me on her lap, and gave me the worst news I ever got in my life.

"Your papa has gone to heaven to be with God," was how she said it. I think now she was trying to make it sound 'okay,' like maybe being with God was a good thing.

4

"I want him to be with me," I screamed as I leapt off her lap and ran to my cot in the corner of her bedroom. I cried for three days, and clung to the sheets so tightly that she couldn't pull me loose.

She let me cry for a while, then eventually she tried to comfort me. "You have to eat," she pleaded.

"I'm going to die so I can be with my Papa," I said. I meant it too.

I must have been a pretty stubborn little girl for a five-year-old. Grandma never could get me to eat until she promised that we would take the bus back to Wilmington so that I could be with my mama and brothers and sister. The storm that had been blowing finally let up and the Greyhound was running again, so we made the trip south. Grandma stayed a few days . . . she slept in Mama's room with her . . . then she left us on our own to try to figure out how we were going to survive. Mama and Amelia did all the figuring.

They decided that Mama would run the store, make the candy, roast the peanuts and cook the wieners. The boys who were old enough, Carl and Albert and Victor, would peddle them in the neighborhood. Amelia decided that it was safe to allow them to go as far east as 16th Street, as far north as Market, south to Greenfield, and west to the river. Albert, the obedient son, always stayed within the lines. And he always sold everything entrusted to him. Carl, and I've never understood why, seemed like a lost soul. He'd drift off to the docks on the river where he'd run with some 'bad elements," as Amelia would call them. It caused him a lot of trouble, and for a while he was sent off to reform school for some theft he was involved in. Victor, short on obedient but long on enterprising, ignored the boundary limits, but nonetheless managed to bring home an empty basket and a pocketful of coins.

Amelia assigned herself the task of running the farm that Papa had east of town. She'd always gone with Papa before he died, and she figured she knew how to manage the Chinese laborers and the planting and the harvest. I think maybe the farm was the most

5

lucrative operation in the Stefano empire. The reason I think that is because, when we lost the farm a year later, the family finances collapsed. But I'll get to that later.

Joe and I, who were too young to make good peddlers, were assigned the task of looking after Fred. Joe, who had no nurturing instincts that I could observe, relied on me to carry out the obligation. I served, but without distinction. Ousted from my throne as my father's princess, I was ill-prepared for day labor. I excuse my behavior now by remembering that I was still not six years old. But I can remember treating Fred in ways that would have earned me a scolding if anyone but me had known my 'trick.'

My 'trick' was this. I'd pull Fred in the wagon down to the river front. It was only a few blocks from home. I'd set Fred looking straight at me, then I'd run toward the docks and pretend that I was going to throw myself into the river. I wanted Fred to plead with me not to, then hug me closely. I wanted to be 'special' again, if not to Papa at least to Fred. It didn't work. Fred just cried. If some psychiatrist reads this someday, he'd probably have me committed. But the statute of limitations has run out on that cruelty, and I've beat myself up for it more than any courts would ever do.

Margaret, Fred and Joe

I did lose Fred one time. For a short while. And I was promptly disabused of the notion that I occupied some special status in our family. Here's how that happened.

Amelia had returned from the farm, a bag of vegetables in tow. That was to be our supper. The boys, Vic and Albert, had returned from their rounds, successful as usual. Carl was absent, but by that time we'd come to expect that. Nobody even mentioned him. We'd all gathered in the kitchen in the rear of the shop, and water was boiling for the corn and the potatoes. Mama had got her legs under her by that time, and she was surveying her brood with evident pride. We were making it. Then a look came on her face. She looked around frantically. "Fred! Where's Fred?" she shouted. Everyone looked at me for the answer. I didn't have one.

Amelia rushed to my side, knelt in front of me, grabbed my shoulders, and repeated Mama's question, "Where's Fred?"

"I don't remember," I admitted. "Somewhere close," I guessed.

Amelia took charge. "Albert, you look east. One block at a time. Victor, you go north. I'll take Joe and Margaret with me and we'll start west, then south if we need to. Mama, you stay here." Nobody argued with her. We all scattered.

It wasn't a very big deal. Amelia spotted Fred. He was in a neighbor's yard, a block away. He had a dirt clod in his hand. He'd crumbled the soft part of it off and was picking at the rest with his tiny fingers.

I later tried to make a joke out of it. "We're so poor we have dirt clods for toys," I invented. No one laughed. Not even me.

Amelia, aka Fluffy

Fred didn't know any of the good times. Not one day of them. He was born too late for that.

If you'd known our family before Papa died, you'd have called us a 'happy family.' That's how Dr. Robert Fales remembered us in the memoirs he published as "Wilmington Yesteryear." "Hard working and industrious people" he called us.

For most of the time that I can remember before Fred was born, our family enjoyed a textbook life.....Papa would say "it'sa good life, Rosa" when she'd mention the old country. Papa was full of energy and ideas. Raising goats on the rocky soils of Casal Cassinese didn't offer the level of opportunity that my father sought. Papa could see farther than the valley that held Casal. He could see farther than the monastery at Cassino that lay at the base of the mountain, and farther than the waters that lapped into the Bay of Napoli nearby. Papa's vision was stretched across the great ocean by his papa, Ferdinando, who had leveraged his charm and musical talents into a globe-spanning adventure.

Grandpa Fernando had been born in Polmonora in 1858. It was a small village a couple of miles from Casal. I think it's gone now, no sign that it had ever existed. His family could not have been very wealthy. Family members who traveled to the area later could find no signs of his forbearers. But it is possible that Grandma's family might have been better off. She told me that they owned a stone quarry, and she described carrying blocks of granite on her head. It's a family mystery, one that will never be uncovered now that the old ones are gone, but somehow Grandpa and Grandma managed to find the resources to travel extensively. Grandma had a sister who lived in

France, and I know they traveled there. I think that's where Papa was born, in Arras. It's also where they departed Europe when they sailed to the United States.

Ferdinando was a musician with a wandering eye and the feet to follow. He would disappear down the road to Aqua Fondata and not return for months. On his travels, 'viaggiari eletrizzante' he called them, he had played his music in the capitals of Europe and South America, and in the biggest cities of the eastern United States. In those days, the waning years of the nineteenth century, that constituted the travel of kings. He'd played more than his violin. Grandma, as stern as Grandpa was enchanting, told me of his wayward tendencies.

"He was with a beautiful woman in every town he visited," She indicted. "He even gave one of them my very best linens. He'd always blame me misplacing them, but I knew the truth. And what was I to do? Trade him for Rico, the smelly butcher? Your grandfather was a charmer...'affascinante.'" I still remember that word jumping off her lips.

I remember when Grandma told me that story, my sympathies lay with Grandpa. It sounded like much more fun. It was only later, when I had come to understand what she had endured, that I realized that she was the rock of the family while Grandpa, the charmer, flitted about the continents.

Their marriage was a stormy one, I heard even violent on occasion. Once, when he'd established the family in Philadelphia, he returned to Italy for a short visit and wasn't seen at home for over a year. Grandma suspected, maybe even knew, that I could well have had half uncles or aunts all along the trail of Grandpa's 'viaggiaris.'

"So why did you marry him?" I asked her one day when we were sitting on her front porch.

"He was very pretty," she answered without a moment's hesitation.

My point isn't Grandpa's indiscretions, or the ups and downs of their marriage. It is that they left the rocky outcropping known as Casal Cassinese, and they experienced a full helping of what the world had to offer. That was how Papa grew up. Born in France; some of his youth spent in Casal, some in Paris, some in Germany. When he was a teenager he sailed with the family from Havre on the La Bretagne to the United States and entered through Ellis Island. From there Ferdinando led them to Philadelphia; to Richmond and Hopewell, Virginia, and then on to Wilmington. Papa traveled back and forth to Italy several times. He married my mother in Casal when he was 20. When I was 8 months old, he returned to Casal from Philadelphia and took us permanently to America. My next three brothers were born there, before Papa pulled up stakes and moved again.

If Papa had lived, and maybe another big 'if,' if he'd had stick-to-it-iveness, we might have been rich. We moved to Wilmington when I was 8 years old. I was Papa's right-hand-man. I helped him with all his businesses. When Papa made the best ice cream in town, I made the best cones. I made them out of cake batter. I'd get up in the morning and make hundreds of them. Then I'd get my white ceramic bowl and Papa would dish me a huge scoop that filled it brim to brim with just-made ice cream. I'd take my finger, poke a hole in the center and pour that hole full of coffee. That was my breakfast for years.

Papa must have become bored with that business, because next he added the meat business. Each morning early we'd go to market where Papa would buy the meat he expected to sell that day. He'd lift me up on the counter to count the change he had coming. He didn't trust that butcher.

We had a good life....decent clothes, plenty of food to eat. We weren't rich. But we got along very well. We had enough money so that each week Papa would give me a dollar for my labor. That was good money in those days. I'd take that dollar and treat nine of my neighborhood girlfriends to the Bijou Theater for the Saturday movies. The Bijou was a big tent, with sawdust floors, and the dollar got all ten of us admitted. I didn't have any trouble being the most popular girl in the neighborhood. The free ice cream I was able to dole out bought a lot of social status.

So there we were, a growing, happy, prosperous family. Mama delivered a baby every two years. I took care of them all, taught them all to walk by holding up their arms and shuffling them along between my legs. They barely had the opportunity to learn to crawl. We laughed; we fought; we ate; we slept; we were family.

And then it happened. Papa took sick. At first it didn't seem like anything worrisome. He'd complain of a sharp back pain when he'd stoop to lift me up on the butcher's counter. I told him I could climb up there by myself, but he told me it was nothing to fret about. But it quickly got worse, much worse. In a matter of weeks he was confined to bed, his fevers and vomiting robbing him of his energy, of himself. When the fever was on him, he turned irritable. I think he began to realize it was out of his control, and he was afraid of what it might mean for the family.

One day, when Mama was in the back making ice cream, he called me up onto the bed next to him. He told me to go to his sock drawer and pull out an envelope that was buried in there. When I handed it to him, pulled out a several bills and gave them to me.

"I want you to enroll at the secretarial school and learn to be a secretary as quickly as you can. We need to get you ready."

"Ready for what, Papa?" I wanted to know. Now he was scaring me.

"We can't run the meat market anymore, Amelia. You'll need a new way to earn money."

"I can run it by myself, Papa," I argued.

"You are an amazing young woman, Amelia, but there are only so many hours in the day. You help your Mama with the younger ones. You help with the ice cream store. But an education as a secretary will be more valuable to you than cutting and selling meat. You do as I tell you." Papa's stern manner told me not to argue anymore.

As Papa's disease got worse, our expenses rose and our income dropped. I continued making the ice cream and the cones in the early morning, then I walked to the secretarial school for my classes. The strain on Mama became too great for her to handle. Caring for Papa was a fulltime job. Grandma took the bus from Columbus to Wilmington, and she took Margaret and Joe back home with her. That lightened the load some. Albert took on a lot of the work around the store. Vic helped what little he could. Carl fell in with some of the rough boys down by the river, and he got himself in a lot of trouble. He finally got caught stealing from a warehouse and was sent to the boy's reform school. I won't say that was a good thing, but at least it was one less mouth to feed, and we didn't have to worry about where he was or what he was up to. We didn't see Carl for a while.

I'm telling all this for one reason . . . to let you know the circumstances that greeted Fred when he was born. I didn't have the time to teach him to walk. Margaret and Joe, the closest in age to him were gone to Grandma's some of that time. Albert and Vic were trying to help with the store. Mama was completely consumed by caring for Papa. It doesn't take much imagination to see him sitting off in a corner, ignored, crying, trying to attract the smallest attention.

But that's not how it was. I don't remember him whining. He didn't cry. He smiled. He was always smiling. Somehow, Fred must have figured that was the way things were supposed to be. He didn't expect anything different and made do with what he could find to entertain himself.

If this next thing had happened today, our family might have been reported to Social Services. One day we actually lost Fred. Well, technically, Margaret lost Fred. But we were all family, and we were all supposed to look after each other, so 'we' lost Fred is probably accurate.

We were all in the kitchen one evening, supper on the stove. It was the usual chaotic scene, Vic tugging Joe's hair; Albert trying to restore order; Margaret acting like a princess who had fallen out of her throne; Mama tending the meal preparation. All of a sudden I realized that something was wrong. I looked around the kitchen....no Fred. I checked every room in the house....still no Fred.

"Margaret, where's Fred?" I demanded. I'm sure my tone was harsh.

Margaret played it innocent. "How am I supposed to know," she parried.

"Because you're the one who's supposed to be watching him," I ran back at her.

"He's around," she finally remembered. 'Where' was not in that sentence.

Well, it turns out he wasn't far. I found him in the neighbor's yard. He was picking at a clod of dirt, a hint of mud on his lips. And he was smiling.

I felt bad that night. I was aware of how baby Fred was lost in the shuffle. I gave him an extra bowl of ice cream that night.

14

Fred

We were all sitting around Fluffy's living room one hot afternoon. It was before she'd gotten air conditioning, and we were arrayed amphitheater-style in front of an oscillating fan, each treasuring the sweep of moving air when it came our way. Fluf was sitting next to the fan, holding court. She'd had her first stroke by that time, so she had her wheelchair aimed at the rest of us. Her voice lacked the power of her earlier years, when a shout from her would reach through the swamp all the way back to the Cape Fear River. Her halting delivery, the stroke's unkind contribution, forced us to pay close attention so that we could understand her measured words. What she lacked in volume and delivery she made up for in conviction, the result being that each of her declarations carried the weight of a first-born's authority. And those accounts swept over us as regularly as the fan's welcome pass.

Vic was in attendance, offering an opinion or observation on every topic. He was not the least bit slowed or intimidated by Fluffy's confident assertions, and commented on every offering, beginning each rejoinder with, "Aw, Fluffy, you don't remember that right at all," followed by his version of that particular event.

Joe was there, sitting in the front row and nodding that sweet smile of his at every utterance. I don't think Joe said a word all afternoon. Frances was with him, but she spent her time shuffling back and forth from the kitchen, making sure everyone had a 'cold sweet tea' to drink. I remember thinking that not even Frances' twenty-year waitress touch could overcome the sulfur taste of Fluf's well water.

Margaret and Mickey were there. Margaret was a pretty good historian, and she was no shrinking violet in offering accounts at odds with both Fluf 's and Vic's. Mickey was taking it all in, this Italian family exchange in colorful contrast to his quieter Lebanese memories.

Carl was there. He sat over by the open door, preferring a breeze to any walk down memory lane. If Carl had any fond memories, I never heard him put voice to them.

Albert had come down for this reunion. He acted as the judge of this event, ruling on the truthfulness or accuracy of each recollection, several variations of which had been asserted as 'the truth.' I don't know if it was his Coast Guard haircut, or his Coast Guard voice, or his Coast Guard bearing, but when Albert declared himself, the crowd seemed to settle on that version as as close to the truth as they were going to get.

Robert and Marguerite were there. The kids were outside playing. No, now that I remember it, Robert had taken the lot of them to Silver Lake for a cold swim. I remember thinking I should have volunteered for that duty. I was on the outside looking in on that afternoon's conversation.

The topic du jour was remembering. Remembering what it was like growing up. Remembering what it was like on Castle Street. Remembering what the store had been like. Remembering what it was like before Papa died. Remembering the kids they played with. Remembering the day the priest came and took us away. I was listening intently. I wanted to know where I came from, and it wasn't going to come from my memory.

Fluf remembered the most. She was the oldest and was like a second mother to the rest of us. She told how Mama had a new baby every two years, and how, as soon as that baby was weaned, Fluf would take over and teach the newest addition how to walk. She said none of us ever learned to crawl. We skipped that stage and went straight to walking.

She remembered a lot about Papa too. She'd worked alongside of him….in the ice cream business; in the meat shop; at the farm Papa had east of town. She remembered a lot of details about each of those experiences. Making the ice cream cones each morning. Going to the butcher and counting change for Papa. The Chinese coolies who worked the fields for Papa. I liked hearing about Papa. I never knew him. Well, to be more accurate, I don't remember anything about him. He died when I was nine months old, and I think he was in bed or the hospital most of that nine months.

I was just too young to remember any of that. Now that I'm older I know from stories what happened. After Papa died, Mama tried her best to keep the family together. She ran the store. She made the ice cream. She made candy. She cooked hot dogs and boiled peanuts. Fluffy and the older boys all helped, selling the treats on the sidewalk and from their wagons. Mama got remarried three years after Papa passed away, to a man named Fred Cisneros. I remember thinking that maybe that might be good for me. It wasn't. Mama had a new baby, Richard, soon after that, and I just got lost in all of that. Cisneros didn't stay around long. I now know that Albert and Fluffy were so mean to him that he left. I recall Fluffy thinking that he only married Mama because he thought her businesses were successful. When he figured out how thin the living was, he disappeared. I don't know if that's true or not.

At some point, I got rescued from all that confusion. The priest from St. Mary's church could see that Mama just couldn't care for the eight of us. Maybe Carl getting sent off to reform school caught his eye . . . I don't know. Vic, Joe and I got taken to the orphanage Nazareth in Raleigh. Vic and Joe were older, and they hung around with older boys. I hardly ever saw them there. I didn't mind that I didn't see them. They always made me feel like I couldn't do anything right, so it was sort of a relief to be in a separate ward.

I loved those years at Nazareth. We slept in one very long hall, the beds spaced every few feet so that there was only enough room between bunks to get in and out of bed. There was no privacy in that dormitory, but the concept of privacy took a back seat to the comfort of the being surrounded by the sounds of the other boys snickering and whispering and tossing and finally sleeping. I think I was the last one asleep every night. I didn't want to miss a single moment of the comfort I felt there. And who knew, maybe she'd come back.

One night, after I'd been there only a short while, Sister Antoinette saw that I was still awake after the other boys had fallen asleep. She probably felt sorry for the new kid, away from his family for the first time. Whatever she was thinking, she came over to my bed, tucked me in, rubbed my sleepy head, and gave me a kiss the forehead.

"Things are going to be just fine, Freddie."

She was the first one that ever called me that. And in that close moment, I learned something else that I decided to keep a secret. The rumor among all the boys was that the nuns shaved their heads and were bald under their habits. Dark as it was, I could see by the dim light from an overhead bulb at the end of the room that Sister Antoinette had long, golden hair. I whispered to her that I didn't know that nuns had regular hair. She put her finger to her lips, in the universal sign for keeping a secret, and she said, "That's just between you and me, Freddie." I felt special, an insider for the first time that I can remember.

I remember getting up each morning and kneeling on the cement floor to say my morning prayers. I remember Sunday mass in the vaulted chapel, the sunlight bursting through the stained glass window. I can even picture the dust motes that floated through the colored beams of light that slanted across the church. I remember the carved Stations of the Cross that drew my eyes from station to station. I remember the magic of the smell of incense as it wafted from the golden censers. I felt very close to God at Nazareth, and that was a very comforting feeling.

I was very smart for my age and so I did very well in my classes. One of my teachers, Brother Dominic, sort of adopted me and took me under his wing. He showed me how to work in the garden, and he taught me the game of 'Doodle-Bug." I'd find an insect hole in the soft earth and lower a blade of grass into the hole, begging the bug to come out into the light. The grass must have been a treat for the bugs because I was usually able to lure one from its den below. I got very good at identifying the various beetles and other insects that inhabited my garden.

There were a lot of children my age at Nazareth, so I was able to play with them as equals, not as the tag-along that my brothers considered me. I couldn't see very well....it turns out that I was later to be diagnosed as nearsighted and blessed with my first pair of glasses.....but I had excellent hand-eye coordination and excelled at horseshoes, mumbly-peg, volleyball, and even football. I was growing quickly and was what one of the brothers called 'quick as lightning.' That made me somewhat of a minor hero as the running back on the football team. Small glory, but enough to satisfy my need for recognition.

When I was old enough I got to become an altar boy and serve mass. I loved reciting the Latin prayers. When I mentioned my interest in Latin, Brother Dominic spent hours after class with me helping me learn Latin. For the first time in my life I was special to someone. Brother Dominic told me that I was destined for great things, and that one day I might even become a priest. I know it sounds strange to say, but I was closer to him than I was to my own family.

I think I could have stayed at Nazareth forever. I could have gone to seminary, become a priest, become a teacher and mentor for other orphans, and lived there for the rest of my life. But that is not how things turned out.

The Depression took its grip on the economy and on people's lives. On my life that meant packing up at Nazareth and being ushered onto a Wilmington-bound Greyhound bus.

The hours of the ride back to Wilmington were the saddest of my life. No, I have to take that back. They were almost the saddest times I ever experienced. Victor and Joe were laughing and wrestling, unable to contain their pure exhilaration. They were sprung from prison and on their way to the sweet freedom of Wilmington's streets. I couldn't imagine how life could go on. I would later come to understand that the Depression showed few favorites as it doled out its abundance of grief to nearly everyone. On that ride the Depression was just a word to me. The face I couldn't drive from my mind was that of Brother Dominic.

Well, I should get back to the family visit in Fluffy's living room that I was describing before. As my brothers and sisters talked about their memories, I could only remember one thing about those early times. I remember ice cream. Every day . . . ice cream. I remember eating ice cream for breakfast, for lunch, for dinner. I didn't think that memory was important enough to warrant mentioning. So I just sat and listened and absorbed the story of my past.

Steve

I see things differently now. I've learned a lot about the times and circumstances that shaped my mother's family, so that now I can paint them with a more diverse palette. But first I want to tell you how they appeared to a teenager.

The summer trips to North Carolina were the highlights of the years that we were able to take those vacations. Grand adventure. The seven of us piled into whatever vehicle my father was driving at the time. The station wagons were the best, but we didn't always have that luxury. Julie rode up front between mother and father. The four boys jostled for prime window seats, a lottery ultimately deciding who got what seat first. We switched after every stop, so the early arguments about who started where were replaced by whose turn it was next. We made a big deal over little things.

The first hours were through relatively familiar territory, southern Ohio. We played cowpoke while we still in farm country, the boys on one side of the car vying to count the most cows on their side until one team reached one hundred. Some counts were more suspicious than others, one brother who shall remain unnamed uncannily able to count the cows in a large herd and come up with numbers the rest of us could not duplicate. Maybe he was a very good counter.

The next miles were through the timbered hills and drew our attention from games to observing.. The bridge over the Ohio River and the sights up and down river were an attraction that made the window seat in that segment of the trip a valuable commodity. The currency of the moment was sourballs....cherry being the most popular, grape second. As the eldest, I held the power, Custodian of the Sour Balls. We opened a can of the hard candy before we left, and it was up to my discretion to distribute them. I cannot now imagine what my parents must have been thinking when they handed me that responsibility. I'm guessing it set me up for a lifetime of brotherly enmity. Point is though, if a guy had a cherry or grape sour ball stashed away, and needed an upgrade to a window seat, the bridge and ensuing mountains and tunnels presented an opportunity for commerce.

The drive took most of two days, so there was always an overnight stay, maybe at Bluefield, West Virginia or Mt. Airy, North Carolina. One trip took us down the spine of the Skyline Drive and the Blueridge Parkway, words that sparked the imagination of a carload of flatlanders. No tender of sour balls could purchase an upgrade to a window seat during that portion of the trip.

I'm not sure what my sister or brothers remember most about those trips. I remember the food. We rarely ate out, so restaurant food was an occasion for exploration. I tended to be adventurous, trying things I hadn't experienced before. Two plates still are as present in my memory as last night's meal......the 'stew beef' special announced on a chalk board above the counter in a ridge top diner in Beckley, West Virginia, and a BBQ pork sandwich, 'southern style,' in Pulaski, Virginia. The stew beef was a deep brown, both in flavor and in color, and it still inspires me to attempt to replicate it. In my continuing efforts, I have yet to burn it crisp enough or dark enough to recreate my memory of that meal. The 'southern style BBQ? . . . no news to a southerner, but Cole slaw piled into the sandwich? . . . that was exotic to a boy used to Catholic school lunches.

But this isn't about travel, or road food, it's about my Italian family. Here's a story that captures a portrait of each of them.

As we were crossing the Piedmont, dropping out of the mountains and through the sandy pine country of North Carolina, the homestretch of a long drive, my mother told us a story that had our eyes wide and our jaws dropped.

23

The family, scattered after her father's death . . . to the Merchant Marine, the Coast Guard, orphanages at Belmont and Nazareth, and points in between . . . had reassembled in the family home on Castle Street. The Depression had forced them back into being a family under one roof. Fluffy and John had returned from Columbus and were living there. Vic and Joe were there, as the unfolding story will reveal. Mag had returned there with Fluffy after completing her high school education in Grandview. And they were all living in the rooms behind the candy store.

One morning, my mother related, Ned the boarder failed to materialize from his room at the far end of the hallway. Vic was dispatched to check on him, and returned quickly to the breakfast table.

"Mawgreet," he directed my mother, "Ned don't appear to be moving. Git on in there and see to him." According to my mother, the entire table then timidly walked down the hall and peered into Ned's room. It's not hard to imagine the scene outside Ned's door.

"You're the big, strong man around here. You go on in there," my mother remembers telling Vic.

Vic was having none of that, and mom finally and hesitantly approached the bedside. She was back outside the room within seconds.

"I think Ned's dead."

The scene that followed Ned's discovery never made it into the family history book, but the 'finding' of Ned was now on record. He had in fact passed away during the night, and my very own mother had bravely entered the room and discovered the body. We arrived at Fluffy's Carolina Beach Road farm soon after that hair-raising story. Hugs and kisses greeted each of us, and within a couple of hours, the calls announcing our arrival had been made and the cars started arriving from town and parking in a circle around the base of the huge oak tree that dominated her yard. Carl and Joyce drove in. Joe and Frances were there. I remember Frances making us all 'sweet tea,' although it tasted like sulfur. Fluffy's water was barely drinkable. We ended up going to town later to fill some bottles with town water. Albert had made the trip down from New London and was in the kitchen busy lining up a 'deep sea' fishing trip. So there we were, all in the house, catching up on each other's lives.

Fluffy, the eldest, most responsible and chairwoman of the board of Stefano Inc. held the spotlight while she told the tale of a recent encounter. Seems she had made a considerable sale of sod and shrubs, had her man Henry load the trailer with the assembled inventory, and she set off toward Calabash where her customer's estate was located. The problem occurred when her Studebaker started across the Cape Fear River draw bridge. There was a tremendous crashing sound just outside her driver side window that "'bout scart me to death," she delivered in her best stage presence.

"I thought I felt somebody run into me, so I pulled over to check the damage. I got out of the car and turned back toward the bridge."

At this point her hands cupped her cheeks in mimed horror. "And what do you think I saw," she moved us to the fronts of our seats.

Waiting just the perfect few seconds for the drama to build, she delivered the goods.

"There was my trailer, its hitch embedded in the radiator of a car that had been passing the other way, steam hissing over the hood. And there, on the pavement were my precious azaleas and stacks of sod, Zoysia Matrella, the king of grasses, to boot. Well, I marched right to that other driver and accosted him."

"Look what you've done to my azaleas," she had begun her tirade.

"Lady," he began his defense, "I didn't do anything to you. Your trailer came loose and crashed into me."

Fluffy paid little heed to his explanation and continued, "I'm a poor widow lady, my only means of support is my landscaping business, and there's my landscaping lying in the middle of the highway." At this point the draw bridge operator had disembarked his pilot seat and approached the building drama.

Sensing an ally with uniformed authority, she turned to him, "Look what this man did to my trailer, and to my azaleas."

The bridge operator, his uniform apparently doing its job, was not about to be distracted by Fluffy's umbrage.

"Lady, your trailer came loose from your car and smashed into this gentleman. And you look at what your trailer has done to my bridge," he momentarily reclaimed the high ground as he pointed to the dented iron side rails.

An ordinary human at this point might have begun to realize her complicity in the carnage. But Fluffy was no ordinary human. As a pre-teen she had helped run her father's business. She had taken charge after his death and managed to get her seven siblings raised. She had married and buried a husband; she'd run a lathe at Camp Davis during the war, turning shapeless metal into meticulously machined gun parts; and she'd supported herself raising and selling grass sod and shrubs along the swamps abutting the Cape Fear. She was undaunted by rattlers, cotton mouths, copperheads and the occasional alligator that invaded her turf, a swift whack of her hoe dispatching any uninvited varmints. This little set-to just needed a little straightening out. She shifted into master sergeant mode.

To the other driver: "You get that trailer out of your radiator and get it hitched back onto my car. And then you get this sod back on there."

To a passer-by who couldn't pass by because of the blocked pavement, a word of practical advice: "This'll go faster if you help him," her pointing to the recently activated and slightly bewildered other driver.

To the bridge operator, an assignment to the most recently discovered component of this debacle: Pointing over the railing, she ordered, "There goes a flotilla of my azaleas, heading down the Cape Fear River toward the ocean. (Fluffy had a vocabulary that made her unbeatable at Scrabble) You git down there and see how many of 'em you can round up. That's my livelihood floating away down there."

And to the building crowd that had been halted by the blocked highway: "You can wait and watch, or you can help get me back on the road."

The miracle of it all was that everyone followed orders without a second thought. Within fifteen minutes the trailer had been rehitched, the sod reloaded, the azaleas rounded up and neatly stacked on the trailer. The bridge operator was in full widow-savior mode as he loaded the last dripping wet azalea onto the trailer.

"How many of them did you have?" He needed to know.

"Thirty-six," she reported.

He shook his head. "Well, you got 42 now," he wrapped up his widow-saving responsibilities for the day. Fluffy, ever the gracious Southern belle, thanked her troops, mounted her steed, and rode off into the sunset, a satisfied legion of collaborators in her wake.

We clapped, cheered, and rolled on the floor with laughter at the 'loaves and fishes' miracle of the Cape Fear River Drawbridge, a staple of Stefano family lore.

That was Fluffy, a formidable fusion of steel and charm.

There was a lull in the stories at that point, possibly because no one felt they could top that production. I didn't have much to contribute, but felt the need to be a part of the event, so when the quiet spell set in, I brought up my mother's heroic tale of finding Ned, a story still fresh in my head.

Fluffy's head snapped around when she caught my drift.

"Your mother told you she's the one who found Ned?" she said in a tone reminiscent of a Perry Mason objection.

"She did find Ned," I confidently came back. My mother was a paragon of truth and virtue.

"No, no, no," Fluffy corrected. "That's not at all what happened." Fluffy then proceeded to tell the story of that eventful morning, a word-for-word retelling of the tale, with one notable exception. In this version, she was the one who emerged from the bedroom with the news, "I think Ned's dead."

Fighting words to my mother. Raised in the confines, mental and physical, of the Belmont orphanage, she'd developed the 'no-authority-too-powerful-to-be-challenged' mindset that was at the center of her spirit.

"What are you talking about, Fluff-Puff," she drilled into her older sister's veneer of invincibility by using a less-than-noble nickname. "You and Vic were standing behind me, pushing me into that room."

The battle was joined. Back and forth they went, no quarter given or asked. Mother Truth was hard to locate in this exchange, and she invited an arbiter into the mix. Enter Albert.

"What's all this fuss, you two?" he interceded as he returned from the phone where he'd been trying to locate an old fishing boat buddy.

Both combatants simultaneously presented their case, drowning each other out and contributing to the overall hilarity of the fracas, much to the delight of those of us in the audience. Albert waded in like a farmer trying to separate two pecking hens.

"Alright you two," he again interrupted. "Fluffy, you go first. Margaret, you'll be next." Order was restored. Fluffy told the story of finding Ned, Margaret fidgeting while truth was being rewritten. Then my mother told her version of the event and it was Amelia's turn to silently fume.

"You both done?" Albert more ordered than asked. His tone answered the question for them. He turned to Joe who was sitting there just smiling.

"Joseph," Albert formally alerted his brother that he was now on the witness stand. "You were there that morning, were you not?"

"I don't remember," Joe judiciously ducked the fray.

"What do you mean you don't remember," Albert accused. "How could you not remember finding a dead man in your house?"

"Then I must'a not been there," Joe tried. Albert knew Joe well enough to abandon that line of questioning. Joe liked to be a part of it, as long as he didn't have to be a part of it. He just sat there listening and smiling.

Albert turned to Carl who was sitting over by the door, looking out to see who might be the next to arrive in the circle driveway.

"Poopdeck," Albert bellowed. "Do you remember anything about that day?"

"What day?" Poopdeck countered as he turned his head toward the proceedings.

"The day Ned died," Albert couldn't believe he had to explain.

"I don't know no Ned," Poopdeck countered. "Hey look, here comes Vic'n Tootie." A red Ford rolled into the driveway,, and that concluded Poopdeck's contribution to the cause of justice.

Poopdeck Pappy....cute nickname; sweet and tired smile; mostly gone and always silent. He was hard to get to know. I later heard he'd been in trouble when he was a kid my age, and that he'd later joined the Merchant Marine, thus his nickname. I've always wondered if he had any interesting stories to tell.

Vic bounded up the stairs with a vigor that attested to his athletic prowess. When Vic arrived in a room, it was the Vic Show until he decided it wasn't. Vic was a plumber when he was sober; a player when he wasn't. According to my mom, who told us these stories when she thought we were old enough to hear them, Vic would work until he'd piled up enough money so that he didn't have to work. Then he and a few cronies and whatever 'party women' he could afford would hole up in the apartment above his shop and play cards and party and drink whiskey and smoke cigars until the money ran out. Then he'd go back to plumbing to start the cycle all over again. Joe used to work for Vic, and that was a big part of Joe's troubles.

Vic had been a very good athlete in his day, probably could have played semi-pro baseball except that it didn't pay as well as plumbing. He owned a baseball team for a while, the Wilmington Pirates, a Class D Tobacco League team. When we got to Wilmington, if the Pirates were in town, we sat in the owner's box. He'd always give us new Louisville Slugger bats, brand new baseballs, cool Pirates hats. It was hard not to like Vic. He was full of life.

He lived next door to a red-headed older kid we played with. He says he taught the kid how to wing a football clean over the shop. I know he could do it. I used to catch him. Sonny Jurgensen went on to play for Duke and the NFL Eagles and Redskins. He's in the Hall of Fame. My uncle Vic taught him how to wing it.

After Vic had made the rounds and said his 'hellos,' Albert reassembled the courtroom and returned to the pursuit of truth and justice.

"We were having a discussion before you arrived," Albert introduced the topic. "We need you to settle something."

Vic liked the challenge. "Roll it out," he invited.

"You were at home the day Ned the boarder died, weren't you?"

"Of course I was home," Vic shot back. "We all were. Remember it like it was yesterday."

"Good," Albert hoped that resolution was within reach. He introduced the preceding events with, "Fluffy claims that she was the one who

31

found Ned, dead." He didn't get out the part about Margaret's similar claim before he was blown backward by Vic's blast:

"Fluffy is the biggest liar on the face of the Earth"…'oit' was how he pronounced 'Earth,' and it took my Midwestern-vanilla ears a moment to translate Vic's version of English into something that I could understand. After a few minutes and some listening adjusting on my part, his Southern slur became intelligible without a hesitating translation step involved.

Albert's shoulders slumped. Then things got worse.

"I was the one who found Ned," Vic proclaimed, launching into Ned's Dead 3.0, again a nearly word-for-word version of the event, except that this time he was the hero of the piece. That of course brought howls of protest from Margaret and Fluffy, and howls of laughter from the rest of us. Except Albert, whose pursuit of truth was in shambles. Joe and Carl, stoics to the core, even hinted at a chortle. Truth was lost in the mists of self-serving memories and further examination was abandoned.

So there you have my mother's family:
Amelia…the family's second mother and She Who Was in Charge.
Albert… the button-down seeker of truth.
Vic…. The promoter, raconteur, bon-vivant and ne'er-do well.
Carl and Joe….quiet observers and,
Margaret…the fiery self-nominated princess of the family.

That leaves out Richard, the half-brother, who had died in a motorcycle accident in the early 40's. We never knew him.

And Fred, who as best I can remember, was never in attendance at any of these family reunions. He was always teaching somewhere…. Mechanicsburg, Cincinnati, Waukegan, Japan. It was almost like he wasn't a part of that family. For a while, he was closer to our family. After World War II was over, Fred, dressed in khakis until he had a chance to shop at Lazarus Department Store for new civilian duds,

came to live with us in Columbus. He and my father's brother Joe, also a returning veteran, were taking advantage of the GI Bill and were enrolled at The Ohio State University. Joe was studying engineering, and I can still see him sitting at the kitchen table, slide rule and protractor at the ready. Uncle Joe was always good for tossing around a baseball or football, and could occasionally be talked into taking us to the Scioto River below Griggs Dam where a young fisherman might tie into a 6 ounce sunfish or bluegill . . . big doin's in those days.

Fred is harder for me to picture. There was no ball-tossing, no fishing. Here's what I do remember. First, opera invaded our house, a serious turn for the worse. Fred assembled a collection of classical records that grew as the months passed. My mother had introduced us to classical music, I particularly remember Peter and the Wolf and a Sibelius symphony that were melodic and comforting, except maybe the wolf part. But opera? That was something else. Caterwauling is the term that comes to mind now. Whenever Fred was in charge of music selection, which included any time mother or father was not at home, he'd uncase an opera selection and fill the house with the most awful screeching. That might explain why my brothers and I became outdoor athletes instead of indoor scholars.

Fred and Joe shared one of the two upstairs bedrooms, my brother John and I the other. My parents set up shop with a bed in the dining room, an amazing testimony to the original version of family values. As our family grew, an expansion of the house to the rear was required to accommodate Michael and Mark, and when Julie came along, I think I remember that she carved out a corner of the room shared by Joe and Fred. Nine of us got the maximum use of that house's one bathroom and one thousand square feet.

A second thing I remember about Fred was his temper. His idea of discipline was one shout and then a whack with the nearest swat-useful object, often a hairbrush. John and I were quick, both at learning and at scampering. We quickly discovered we could outrun Fred, scrambling up the stairs and into the bathroom which provided a locked door and a safety shelter until Fred's temper had cooled and he had returned to whatever he was doing before.

Fred had one more memorable characteristic. Fred sat at the end of the table opposite my father, a strategic post from which he could observe and reach every plate. Fred would start doing the calculus early in the meal, estimating what portion of food each eater was likely to finish. He ate, maybe I should say inhaled his food early in the meal, casting a greedy glance at every other morsel aplate. It was just a matter of time, when Fred had judged that a particular eater had slowed sufficiently, that he would pop the question, "Are you going to finish that.....(fill in the blank)." If there even a moment's hesitation in the reply, Fred's arm would reach out and snatch the plate, and with a flash of fork, clear it clean. Fred was the Black Hole of Food. No morsel, no scrap of fat, no crust of bread ever made it to the garbage heap. Fred was the stomach of last resort, the cleaner of plates, the salvation of children who didn't like their spinach. No starving child of Europe ever would have been appalled by food wasted at our table. If we learned one thing from Fred, it was this: if there are seconds to be had, it paid to eat fast. But no matter how fast we were, Fred was faster. We could have made a fortune renting him out to dieters.

Eventually Fred graduated with Bachelor and Master's degrees in Classical Languages, a favorite of the Classics Department, and we were none too sorry to see him off to his first teaching job. Julie inherited the freed-up bedroom, the opera quotient was substantially reduced, and we were left with just one Italian temper in the house. The bathroom refuge was still occasionally employed.

So what did Fred look like to a young nephew? He wasn't much fun to be around. He wasn't easy to get to know. He couldn't or wouldn't toss a ball. He wasn't like us, wasn't interested in the same kinds of things. But you could count on him to finish your liver.

Fred

If I had picked my own nickname, I'd have chosen "Sunny." I know it doesn't sound very masculine, but it reflects how I saw myself. Dictionary definition.... 'bright and cheerful.' Fred definition..... 'regardless of the circumstances, I can choose to be bright and cheerful. People like me better that way.' I figured that out early.

I'd have liked 'Sonny,' but nobody ever called me that. Not Papa, who'd died before I ever got a chance to know him. Not Mama, who had her big boys: Carl, Albert, Victor and Joe; and her new favorite, Richard, who drew all her attention.

Instead I got stuck with "Quick as Lightning...'Quick' for short." That was because I was the fastest runner at Nazareth.

The title 'Sunny' would have been sorely tested during the Depression. The capital "D" version meant the one the world's economy was experiencing. That one didn't bother me very much. I had everything I needed at Nazareth: plenty of food, a cozy place to sleep, and best of all, I was special there. I was on my way to becoming one of God's chosen servants. I was destined for big things. I even dared dream of sainthood.

The small 'd' depression was my own personal hard time. It started one day when Brother Dominic took me aside after morning Mass. I was hanging up my cassock and surplice and was headed for breakfast when he motioned me to wait a moment. I knew something was wrong by the expression on his face. It wasn't the usual 'jolly' look that was his trademark.

"I have something to tell you, Freddie," he worked his way toward what he needed to do.

"We got a call from the bishop yesterday," he inched forward. "These are hard times. The faithful don't have as much to share with us as they used to," he veered slightly as he tried to sugar coat what was to follow.

"We can't keep you with us anymore," he finally landed the punch to the stomach that he'd been ordered to deliver. I reeled backward as violently as if it had been a real roundhouse blow. It took me a moment to steady and straighten myself. When I had, I could see him wince, and I tried to recover, to spare him what I knew was as painful for him as it was for me.

"What does that mean?" I needed to clarify the dimensions of this announcement.

That question allowed Brother Dominic the opening to shift the responsibility to an impersonal universe, or at least to a higher-up representative of that cosmos.

"The bishop has the care of his entire flock to consider," he was now more safely on the logical track of his mission. He'd rehearsed this part a dozen times.

"He has concluded that the Church no longer has the resources to tend to all in need, so he must make the decision on who are his most vulnerable charges."

"You're one of the lucky ones, Freddie," he offered, unconvincingly, both to me and to himself. "You have a family to return to," he named the source of my good fortune.

"Many of the children here at Nazareth have no one." I knew that part was true.

"There has to be some kind of mistake," I countered. "Does the bishop realize that I am committed to becoming one of his servants, committed to the priesthood?"

"It didn't enter into the bishop's decision," Brother Dominic swiftly and cleanly discounted the core of my being. I'm not sure any words ever hurt me more.

"I'm a hard worker," I tried to extend the fight. "I can more than earn my keep."

"I'm sorry, Freddie. There's nothing I can do. The bishop has spoken and that's the final word."

"The final word." I'd hear that phrase years later, and it would push me onto a new path, more me and less Church in defining my own faith.

"What's going to happen to me?" I accepted my fate, at that time entrusting such a precious asset to a higher authority.

"Father Kelly will be taking you to the bus station tomorrow morning. You'll be home by afternoon," he tried to cheer me.

"Home?" I thought. *"Nazareth is my home."*

It's probably an exaggeration to say I was depressed during my Wilmington years. I'd had little memory of it before I arrived at the bus station, so I had no expectations of what it might be like. I still harbored the dream of sainthood via the priesthood, and Father O'Brien (I hoped you didn't have to be Irish to become a priest, but I'd yet to meet an Italian one) encouraged me by assigning me to the first string altar boy team. Actually there was no first string altar boy team, that was a self-awarded honor, but I was always assigned to the big Masses, the ones where the church was full. My booming voice and my gifted pronunciation of the Latin responses made me a natural for that stage.

I was, however, quickly promoted to the first string football team at St. Mary's. As I said before, I got my growth early, so I outweighed many of the other boys by a good thirty pounds. That size and my natural speed caught the eye of Coach Ryan (again the Irish authority), and I was elevated to the team's fullback role. The Coach heard my nickname, 'Quick,' and he decided it needed fiercified.

"From now on," he commanded the team, "you call Fred here 'Crusher.'"

To me his orders were just as direct. "Fred, Crusher, from now on I want you to run right over anyone who's trying to tackle you. Break some bones. Protestant bones at that," he sweetened the pot, assuming that I shared his ill will toward the unsaved.

That seemed wrong to me. The unsaved included boys from Castle Street, boys that cheerfully shared space and interests with me and our family, and the idea of trying to hurt them was not in my nature. Plus, no one had money for doctoring if it were needed. It was simpler to juke and sidestep them than to argue the point with the coach, and as long as the yardage and touchdowns piled up, he seemed at least tolerant of my bestowing a little of God's mercy on the heathens. It was a different kind of 'special,' and the long-term path to my eventual sainthood less evident, but 'special' at something trumped 'special' at nothing.

Staying "Special" turned out to be more complex the following season. I enjoyed the popularity that came with my running prowess. People knew who I was and wanted to be my friend. My brothers even showed some signs of accepting me as a 'man.' One afternoon, before a crucial game, Coach Ryan called me aside.

"Crusher," he began, "I've got a special assignment for you," a promising introduction to what would turn out to be a not-so-promising directive.

"Their quarterback is also their linebacker."

"I know," I interrupted, "Tommie Taylor, he's a neighbor of mine." I don't think Coach Ryan knew that. The new information didn't deter him from his mission.

"I am going to run you right at him....every play. I want you to put your helmet down and run right over him, no dodging, no juking. I want you to hit him so hard he wants go home. Understand? I want you to take the fight of him real early in the game."

Here's where my path to sainthood took a wrong turn. I followed Coach Ryan's order with no moral filter invoked. On our first offensive play the coach called my number on an off-tackle left run. The linemen opened a hole big enough for me to dart through, and there in my path stood Tommie Taylor, his shoulders squared and his feet planted, ready to take me down. I know I could have made a quick feint and sidestepped him, creating a clear and unguarded path to the end zone. I didn't juke. I lowered my helmet, as per instructions, and caught Tommie just under his helmet with mine. He'd raised his arms to protect himself when he realized that I was coming straight at him, so his left forearm took the full weight of my blow. I heard the bone snap, a memory that I'll never erase. He keeled over backward landing flat on his back. The collision knocked me off balance and I stumbled to the ground a few yards past Tommie's prostrate figure. I sat there for a moment, slightly dazed myself. My helmet was sitting cockeyed on my head and as I tried to straighten it out, I realized that I had split it in two, right down the middle. It must have made a bizarre sight, angling outward from my ears and held together by only the chin strap. I unsnapped the strap and tossed the useless helmet to the ground. It was then that I turned back toward the line of scrimmage and saw Tommie flat on the ground, his arm drawn to his chest and his moans audible clear to Castle Street.

40

The coaches tended to Tommie, putting a splint on his broken arm before taking him off the field and directly to the Cape Fear Hospital emergency room. While Tommie was being attended to, I was being silently congratulated by Coach Ryan and my teammates. Even Vic was in attendance, the game having some city-wide significance, and he patted me on the back, not to console me but to recognize my manly deed.

I sat on the bench, torn between the two competing emotions.....praise on the one side, shame on the other. Shame won in a rout. I finished the game, juking and cutting my way to three touchdowns and never letting a defender so much as touch me. I turned in my uniform at the end of the game, a complete bafflement to Coach Ryan and my brothers. I wanted to be liked, to be accepted, but not at the expense of Tommie Taylor or anyone else. I couldn't imagine hurting someone on purpose. I had a hard time looking Tommie in the eye after that, even though he dismissed my apology with "It's part of the game" . . . and then he added with a twinkle, "Crusher."

My hero status was quickly withdrawn, at school and at home, a casualty of my unexplained and sudden retirement. Word spread that I was 'chicken,' afraid to take a hit. I didn't figure I'd improve my reputation by admitting that I didn't want to hurt anyone. I concluded that it was time for a new plan.

I say plan. Actually it was more of a drift. I gravitated toward spaces where I was comfortable and where I'd found I could be special again. I turned my energies to academics, including an emphasis on Latin, which was miraculously available to me in Wilmington. My teacher, Mrs. Powell, seemed to be surprised and heartened by my interest and performance, her approval being about the only accolade I could earn. At home mother was wrapped around Richard's little finger. Vic, Carl and Joe were dismissive of their 'chicken' little brother. My help in the store earned my keep bit little else.

As I hear myself describe those years, it sounds like a 'poor me' recitation. That would leave the completely wrong impression. I'll admit that I liked the attention I received as a star runner, although not at the ultimate price exacted by Coach Ryan. But my newfound anonymity had its rewards as well. I was freed from wanting or needing the approval of others. I could make my own happiness. I had the time and space to indulge my passion for reading. I was a fixture at the public library, devouring every book I could get my hands on. I met a host of new and lifelong friends. Cervantes introduced me to a new hero, Don Quixote, who became my role model. Marlowe gave me Dr. Faustus and Tamburlaine and Dido, Queen of Carthage. I read every word of Thomas Wolfe and Fyodor Dostoevsky; of Charles Darwin and Thomas Hardy and Joseph Conrad; of Boccaccio and Cellini. There weren't enough hours in the day to read all that I desired. My world grew. My interests expanded. The candy store and my brothers plumbing business seemed tiny compared to the world I inhabited; my friends infinitely more complex and inspiring than theirs. Many of my family and peers thought I was crazy for spending all my time with my nose buried in a book.

But not everyone. With the money I had earned I bought a present for everyone in my graduating class of 1937. And they didn't think I was crazy; they chipped in the $4 it took to buy me the Works of Shakespeare, illustrated by Rockwell Kent. I treasure it to this day, both for the genius of The Bard, and for the understanding of my classmates.

The graduation ceremony that June brought another warming memory. I was wearing a new suit that Fluffy had sewed for me. My sparkling white shirt and red tie were presents sent from Margaret. They wanted their little brother to look sharp for the big occasion.

Mama, dressed in her finest attire, accompanied me to the senior banquet and dance. It was held at the Cape Fear Hotel, not the usual Knights of Columbus Hall. Big doings, I'll tell you. Mama looked so pretty. Several of my classmates commented on how swell she looked.

I think that made her feel good. I thought she'd leave after the banquet, but she was having so much fun watching the young folks frolic that she stayed until the last dance. Mrs. Powell was so kind to Mama and stayed right next to her all evening, telling her stories about each of us. And I did get one special mention that day....my diploma was ablaze with a gold Cum Laude seal. I'd trade that for All-City Fullback honors any day. That is one day I remember as clearly as if it were yesterday.

A few months later Millie, who had gone back to Columbus for a while, returned to Wilmington and bought the grass farm on Carolina Beach Road. All of us boys helped clear the barn out, starting by running out all the snakes. The old floor was dirt, and we hauled and finished concrete until we were exhausted. Good thing it was winter. If it had been during the summer's heat, I don't know if we'd have made it. Fluffy then set to finishing the upstairs, the place she'd call home for the rest of her life.

Margaret stayed behind in Ohio, installed in a new job and dating a fine young man, Mickey, who she would soon marry. John Biddle was too sick to travel, and he stayed in Columbus, cared for in the county sanitarium. John's deteriorating health was a worry to us all. I remember Mama cajoling all us boys to reach into our pay envelopes and contribute five or ten dollars that she could send north to Columbus to help out John or Margaret. Vic and I were easy touches, never having to be asked twice. Mama's sermon on the need for the family to stick together and share what we had fell on deaf ears with Carl, and he was a little hard to find around payday. As best I can remember he rarely added anything to the few bills slipped into an envelope and mailed to my sister.

I have one other clear memory of those years. Franklin Delano Roosevelt was our president and he was leading the country out of the Depression. I sat by the radio in the store and listened to every word he spoke. He seemed like our savior, like the savior I learned to love and wanted to serve as a priest. I scribbled furiously trying to catch each thought. Here are three that I copied onto an index card and still carry in my wallet with me:

The test of our progress is not whether we add more to the abundance of those who have much; it is whether we provide enough for those who have too little.

Democracy cannot succeed unless those who express their choice are prepared to choose wisely. The real safeguard of democracy, therefore, is education.

Human kindness has never weakened the stamina or softened the fiber of a free people.

He was telling me that the things I valued most, kindness and caring and education, were important. I needed to hear that and have my own growing sense of confidence reinforced. I vowed that I would march to his calling.

Front Row: Carl, Richard, Fred. Center: Mama   Back Row: Albert, Vic, Joe.

That's about all I can remember from that time in Wilmington. A few years later I moved to Columbus to join Margaret. The Ohio State University offered a treasure of courses in the Classics and I wanted to develop the skills to be able to help my country become the place that the president envisioned.

The war intervened and gave me a new definition of service. I wasn't looking back to Nazareth anymore. I had a new place where I could connect, where I could be part of something, where I could contribute, where I could be in service to my president. The Army Air Corps became my new home.

<u>Fred</u>

Adjusting to army life became a whole new challenge. The sergeants reminded me of Coach Ryan, yelling and screaming and demanding absolute and immediate obedience to their authority. That didn't feel right to me. I wanted to be a good soldier, to be accepted as part of the team. But something inside of me rebelled at the thought of surrendering my independence, my soul I reasoned, to someone else. In my bunk at night in the barracks I tossed and turned as I wrestled with dilemma this posed. When I mentioned my quandary to another recruit, Harold Steed who I remember was from Zanesville, he just said, "Fred, you think too much."

I walked back through my experiences, looking for lessons that might help me sort this out. Reliance on the authority of the bishop at Nazareth resulted in a long, lonely bus ride, booted unceremoniously into the unknown, not exactly an endorsement of trusting a higher power to look after my interests. Following Coach Ryan's directives steered me to a collision course with my conscience, my conscience ultimately winning that encounter at the price of a bone in Tommie Taylor's forearm. The score at that point was Authority 0, Fred 2.

I remembered a quote I'd read from George Bernard Shaw; I'd copied it onto an index card: "The reasonable man adapts himself to the world. The unreasonable one persists in trying to adapt the world to himself. Therefore all progress depends on the unreasonable man." I counted that as another vote for maintaining as much of a sense of myself as the environs permitted.

Turned out Steed had a point. In the end circumstance trumped philosophy and I was able to be me without having to cross any ethical or principled lines. It's not that I didn't think it was an important debate to have with myself. It's just that my path never crossed a situation where I had to act in opposition to who I was. I might add here that my brother Joe wasn't as lucky, or maybe as contemplative. In his infantry unit he was assigned to the business end of a flamethrower, and he lived the rest of his days with the images of his actions seared into his mind and soul, changed forever. Gentle Joe was a casualty of fate's dictates. That said, I could never have pulled that trigger.

Fate's first blessing on me was assignment to an Army Air Corp weather reconnaissance squadron. I didn't need killer tendencies to play my role in that unit. All I had to do was follow orders. RUN.....I could run faster than anyone else in the company. MARCH...I could march all day long. POLISH THOSE BOOTS....I could see my reflection in the boot tips. PUSHUPS.....I could do 100 without breathing hard. PULL UPS....Same thing. So I got along in basic training with little trouble. I actually enjoyed the exercise.

A couple of incidents during training helped shape my MOS, Military Occupational Specialty. The first hint of the limits to my death-dealing capacity came one day when I was in my tent, cleaning my freshly-issued rifle. I probably was doing something wrong when the gun discharged, nearly taking off my nose. It shot a hole in the roof of the tent. Immediately alarms started going off and soldiers were rushing everywhere, grabbing their rifles and preparing for who knows what. The sergeant quickly figured out what had happened, called off the alarm, and got right in my face.

"Jesus Christ, Stefano," the sergeant screamed, his nose two inches from the one I nearly sent skyward, "Give me that thing before you get somebody killed." He snatched it unceremoniously from my shaking grip. The other recruits had a hard time keeping a straight face.

"I didn't know it was ready to shoot," I protested.

He stepped back, looked at me incredulously. "Ready to shoot? Did you just say, 'Ready to shoot?'"

"Yes sir," I replied in a less than booming voice.

"That would be 'loaded' in Army parlance, Stefano, locked and loaded."

I was impressed by his vocabulary. His heretofore Neanderthal nature inclined me to underestimate him.

"As you were, Stefano," he ordered as he backed off, my rifle now confiscated. "I'll need to give this some thought."

It was quite a while before he reissued me a weapon.

The second occurrence that shaped my career could have been equally detrimental to my health. We were being introduced to the P-38, the mainstay of the squadron's fleet. I'm still not sure what I could have been thinking or where my attention was, but all of a sudden the sergeant tackled me to the ground. We were now side by side on the concrete, noses again two inches apart.

"Jesus Christ, Stefano," came the now familiar preface, "You just about walked into that propeller. Are you trying to get yourself killed?"

Wherever my mind had been, it was now retrieved to the moment.

"No sir," I replied. I think I also issued a quiet 'Thank you.'

My reputation was growing by the day. Our talents eventually measured and charted, I was assigned to an office position, assistant, actually secretary, to the squadron commander, Major Dyas. My conscience wouldn't be challenged by my encounters with a typewriter or file cabinet.

The Major took a liking to me. There were times when we engaged in conversations, person to person rather than major to enlisted man, and I think he enjoyed the range of topics that we were able to discuss. He was a well read gentleman, and in quiet moments we chatted about Dostoevsky's works, Puccini's operas, Beethoven's symphonies. My occasional insertion of Latin phrases particularly tickled him.

That relationship came in handy one week. We had been paid the previous Friday and three really nice guys offered to take me into Winston Salem with them, to 'show me a good time.' We went to bar after bar, downing beers and shots. The adventure lasted three days and nights. I don't remember any sleep, although there must have been interludes where we stopped to catch our breaths. It was my first experience over that line, and I don't remember any of the details.

Except this one. When we got back to Morris Field, my pay envelope was empty, my head hurt like I'd butted head with a buffalo, and I was officially AWOL. Apparently my pass had run out two days before. I was awarded temporary quarters in the base brig and was sitting on a cot wondering how I'd gotten myself into this jam and how I was going to get out, when Major Dyas came into the cell.

49

"I'll take Stefano with me," he ordered the corporal on duty. When we got back to his office, he gave me a father-to-son lecture.

"Fred, your buddies were more interested in your pay than your welfare. You might want to stick closer to base in the future."

My introduction to the world of sin, venial though it may have been, was all the education I needed in that curriculum.

In September of that year, 1942, we boarded a train and headed north to Fort Dix, New Jersey. Training was over and we were heading for the front, although which front was still a mystery to us. The mood in the squadron was still light....we were on a great adventure at this point, out to defeat the Jerrys, everything ahead of us the unknown. A few days passed uneventfully as we sat around the barracks and traded speculation on what might be next. Finally the orders came and we gathered our barracks bags, helmets, overcoats, field packs and rifles (I now had one), and after a three hour train ride and a short ferry trip, we boarded the troop ship, made our way through the maze of halls and compartments, and finally found our assigned cabin, outfitted with triple-decker bunks, eighteen of us to that room. As we slipped into our narrow notches, someone in the room said, "Hey, this is the Queen Mary." If I'd been warmer or more awake, that might have been an exciting discovery. As it was, I was asleep before the echo of his revelation had drifted silent.

Quarters were cramped and stuffy so many of us spent both day and night on deck, curled up under our overcoats to shield us from the blustery Atlantic chill. Five days out of New Jersey, as we cut our way through the gray seas, I had gone below deck to escape the crowded deck when there was this sudden, dull but very distinct thud. I thought that we'd been hit by a Jerry torpedo. I clambered through the hallways and made my way to the deck. Soldiers were crowding the rail in eerie silence.

"Have we been hit?" I needed to know

"We just hit a British cruiser," one of the men was able to get out. "She cut right across our bow. We hit her, she sliced in two, and sank just like that. I don't think any of the poor devils got out alive."

That story never made it to the newspapers or radio until the war was over. According to a report on the incident that was later published, the Queen Mary wheeled to starboard to escape a suspected U-boat; the cruiser veered sharply to port to deal with the sub. The collision tore a gaping hole in the QM, and the cruiser sank within a minute with all hands lost.

We lost several hundred of our allies that day. We lost our innocence. This was no longer fun. The war was now more than an idea. It was real, almost surreal.

That night the cold and drizzle drove us below decks, and when we climbed out into the open air of the morning, we found ourselves surrounded by gray might.....battleships, aircraft carriers, cruisers, corvettes, cargo ships, troop transports......what seemed like the world's entire navy. Beyond the flotilla we could spot the craggy coast of Scotland. Dry land never looked so good.

A train carried us south to Wattisham where we spent the next few weeks wondering what was next, with an occasional dive into bomb shelters when Jerry planes would attack the base. No one was hurt, some of the bombs being duds, but it served to underscore that we were now in the war, not at war. In late October again we were herded onto the trains and headed back north to Scotland, We boarded the ship "Letitia" and the next morning slipped out of the harbor. We were at sea for two weeks, heading to destination unknown until one afternoon a British officer addressed us. I won't forget his words.

51

"You won't become good soldiers until you have become 'blooded', until you've seen men die and until you have killed men. All good soldiers are 'blooded.'"

That speech set off another frenzy of introspection... "Could I actually ever kill anyone?" I thought not.

If it was unsettling in that respect, his talk did clear up one mystery. He then proceeded to distribute our supplies, which included head nets, mosquito cream and a small blue book entitled "North Africa." One question at least had a definite answer.

We landed in Algeria, greeted by sirocco winds and stinging red dust. During the next two months we set up and tore down our camps at least a half dozen times, arriving finally in French Morocco. Without a shred of news of how the war was going or what we might be asked to do, we were kept occupied setting up tents and tearing them down while were waiting for our aircraft to arrive. Our camps were rows of pup tents, set up on a grid pattern designed to minimize any damage that could be done if enemy bombers attacked. The daily air raid drills, a shrieking siren followed by our mad dashes to the bunkers we had dug into the African soil, became so matter of fact that the one time we actually were under attack, the few bombs that exploded around us almost seemed like a part of the drill. Absent any clear mission or enemy encounters, it felt more like Boy Scout camp than a war.

The camps were frequented daily by a hoard of Arab youngsters, picking up any scrap of food or waste that they were lucky enough to happen upon. They were trying to figure out how to survive while the Germans and now the Americans carried out our war in their land. I felt sorry for the poor ragamuffins and at first tried to share some of my supplies with them. It became obvious immediately that my minuscule efforts were futile, a bigger problem than I could solve with my meager stash of gum and candy.

In December the squadron was reunited when our A-20s arrived. Their route had taken them from Florida south over Brazil, across the South Atlantic to South Africa, then north across the African continent and the Sahara to our base. They lost 13 of the 36 craft that had begun the journey, not to enemy fire but to weather and mechanical issues. These were the first casualties our squadron had suffered, a portent of a future bloodier than our service so far. For the next month the aircraft flew routine sub patrol missions while I kept my typewriter smoking. I did draw an occasional night of guard duty, and did it all well enough to earn a promotion to corporal.

In January we moved again, this time to the very eastern border of Algeria, our mission now to support ground operations in Tunisia by spotting enemy movement and location. We were now within a few miles of the enemy and our long months of waiting and preparing were over. This time we set up our tents in any gully or depression we could find. Any sirens from now on meant we were under attack.

The hardest element to deal with was not the rain, not the cold, not the mud, not even the occasional raid by German fighters. The hardest thing was the lack of information....we ran on rumors, not data. One moment we were being briefed on Plan B, our evacuation route should Rommel break through the Kasserine Pass. The next day were moving out again, this time to take over the base that he'd just been occupying. We didn't know if we were winning the war or losing it. The patriotic fervor that we'd felt upon our enlisting into the service had been replaced by the certainty of uncertainty....we knew virtually nothing about the larger context. We just knew today's orders, and the wisdom that finally grew to be our theme song...."War is ninety percent waiting"

We did know we were now at the front. Daily missions over enemy territory made the return of our planes and crews the focus of all our attention. When one of 'our boys' went down, the sadness pervaded the entire camp. We truly were like brothers by that point. By April the Germans had been driven to the very northeast tip of Tunisia, and by May those who hadn't been killed or captured had retreated across the Mediterranean, with the Allies in hot pursuit. Our squadron moved back across Algeria and began training for future reconnaissance missions while our troops assaulted the island-hopping retreat of the Germans and Italians, first Pantelleria, then Malta and finally Sicily. On September 3 the BBC broadcast the news that Italy had unconditionally surrendered. There was a lot of whooping and cheering in camp that night, and new questions began to swirl....where would we go next?

While we waited for orders, I got to know a number of the Italian prisoners who seemed glad to be finished with their portion of the war. They treated us more like liberators than conquerors. Because of my Italian heritage, they talked openly with me.

"La guerra...fini presto," they'd say. I hoped they were right.

Then rumors of momentous events followed one after another. Roosevelt and Churchill are meeting with Chiang Kai Shek in Cairo! Then Roosevelt and Churchill are in Teheran to consult with Stalin. Our confidence was building that we might soon end this war. But first, more waiting.

In mid-January we finally boarded the "George G. Meade" and sailed east along the north coast of Africa, the convoy growing as we sailed. By the first of February we entered Naples harbor and anchored there for two nights and days. Instead of the imagined hail of gunfire associated with an army's landing on the enemy coast, we were greeted by a flotilla of rowboats, manned by enterprising Italians who wanted to conduct commerce.

"One pack cigarettes," they'd shout, pointing to their offerings of baskets of oranges, apples, walnuts, cabbages, cauliflower, carrots, radishes, wine, cognac and souvenirs. The floating markets continued unabated until darkness closed up shop.

One particularly bold and buxom signora put on a show for the entire crew, or at least those who were able to elbow their way to a prime spot at the ship's railing. At the price of four packages of cigarettes, she bared her breasts and had cameras popping and the crew hooting and clapping in appreciation. The following day she reappeared and for another four packs of the prized weed, she repeated her performance, earning herself the nickname 'The Waterfront Dairy.' I don't want to sound prudish, but I had a hard time understanding how a glimpse of a woman's breasts, from the distance of maybe 50 yards, could arouse such a spontaneous outburst from our crew. The sight of Vesuvius looming over the city in the background seemed a more thrilling object of our attention.

Our raucous welcome to Italy ended when we left the ship and were trucked to a temporary shelter where we bivouacked overnight in what had been before the war a school for crippled children. That evening we were in for a surprise, that being that we were actually informed of our mission without weeks of waiting. Our major called us together for a briefing and informed us that we were being assigned to the Fifteenth Air Force Headquarters and would be leaving in the morning for Bari, a town on the southeast coast of Italy. My sketchy knowledge of Italian geography was enough to convince me that our path would take us across the Apennines near my parents' home village of Casal Cassinese. I wondered at that possibility, and at what Papa might have thought about his son's return to 'the old country.' I know he would not have been proud of his country's role in that war. That trip, with dozens of us crammed into the back of a tarpaulin-covered truck, was the coldest, bounciest, most miserable time of any of my service to God, country and FDR. By the time we reached Bari, I had completely forgotten about any thought of Casal. I just wanted to find a warm spot where I could thaw out.

Turns out the Italian prognosticators weren't even close. 'La Guerra' was nowhere near 'fini.' It was, however, 'la guerra.' We were no longer bit role players. We were flying daily missions as the Allies drove northward through Italy toward the German homeland. In May the Germans evacuated the demolished ruins of Cassino, which it turns out was only a short downhill drive from Casal Cassinese. I never did make it there. By June we'd driven them from Rome. A month later newly-minted Sgt. Fred Stefano was granted a four day leave and a group of us toured Rome like tourists, hitting all the must-see sights. We, along with thousands of others, even had an audience, albeit a large one, with the pope. We kept hoping that this series of defeats would weaken the enemy and hasten surrender. Instead we got an increasing barrage of propaganda announcing new secret weapons that they were preparing to unleash on us. Flying bombs was the rumor, and they were in fact able to launch enough V-2s to make the threat credible.

We each found our own way to live through this series of roller-coaster emotions. We could relieve the stress of our mission and go into Bari on our passes. Some of the men traded their cigarette rations for the favors of willing and desperate signoras. My lusts were quenched when I discovered that I could trade a bar of soap for a dozen eggs, and that Mama Stoppani and her daughters would cut me a bargain, half of my eggs for a sumptuous omelet. This post, if closely engaged in the actual fighting, was actually a very pleasant place to fight a war. Our crews flew daily missions, weather permitting, in support of our northward push. We scouted and attacked the oil fields of Ploesti, the ports in Vienna, the storage depots in Bucharest. Our eyes scoured the skies for evidence of our returning crews. Many days the news was sad....another pilot and plane lost. Another winter came and went. Early 1945 brought renewed hope that the European war would soon be over, but that was accompanied by a new alarm, that many of us would be moved into the Pacific theater.

The roller-coaster dipped. In May we were shattered by the news of the death of FDR, a man we'd come to believe was invincible. His death raised new questions about who would be making the big decisions...Stalin? Churchill? Truman? . . . . ..who was he? In June it shot straight skyward when the Germans surrendered. It dipped again as May, June and July were filled with rumors about what lay in store for us. Finally we received news that the defense department had developed a formula based on how long we had been engaged in the war efforts. Our entire squadron had achieved the required 85 points that meant we'd be returning to the United States and discharges. No jungles of the South Pacific for us.

After a few last trips into Bari, for eggs or other, we boarded the USS Argentina and ten days later drew into New York harbor. The sight of Lady Liberty was as welcome to us as it must have been to my father and mother forty years earlier. I was ready for a new life, one closer to a daily shower and regular hot meals. I boarded a train bound for Columbus Ohio where Margaret and Mickey had a room and a spot at the dinner table waiting for me.

Fred

The Ohio State University was a crowded place in 1945. GIs returning from the war and anxious to get on with their lives flocked to the halls of higher education to take advantage of the GI bill. I was one of the flock. But I needed some new feathers.

Flush with my final pay envelope I took the bus downtown to the Lazarus Department Store and traded my well-worn khakis for new civilian threads. Margaret said I looked sharp. Mickey praised the look with his trademark utterance, "KissKissoo." I couldn't find that in the dictionary, but I knew it meant something good.

I enrolled in September of 1945 and found two new homes. One was 1281 Oakland Avenue in Grandview, Margaret and Mickey's place. Joe Buttress, Mickey's youngest brother, returned to Columbus from his service in Germany about the same time and we took over their bedroom on the second floor of the 950 square foot home. Joe was enrolled in the engineering college and spent many an evening hour hovering over the kitchen table, slide rule, protractor and drawing instruments at the ready.

Stephen and John, who were 4 and 2 at that time, slept in bunk beds in the other bedroom on the second floor. Margaret and Mickey gave up their privacy, hung a green retractable drape between the living room and the dining room, and set up camp on a double bed in the main dining room of the house. It's still amazing to me how families coped in those days, sharing space and table and support.

I remember thinking 1281 was crowded until we took a Sunday drive Mickey's family home in Cambridge. That house was no bigger than

1281, and it was shared by Albert, Hafifi, George, Naz, Aneese, Joe, Betty and Rose . . . I thought. One day we were sitting around, before Sunday dinner was served and before the obligatory bridge game had started, when I asked how they'd all fit into such a small space. Betty explained it. Grandma and Grampa had the front bedroom upstairs. Rose and she had the middle bedroom. The boys all slept around the coal stove in the living room.

"What about the third bedroom upstairs?" I asked.

"Oh," Betty casually replied, "that's where the boarders stayed."

And oh yes, the bathroom for all eight Buttresses, plus however many boarders there were at any given time, was a short walk back to the red-painted privy on the alley, next to the shed where the chickens were raised and the garden tools stored.

Millie and John had originally owned 1281, but sold it to Mickey and Margaret when John became fatally ill and Millie was forced to return to Wilmington. It was a wonderful home, tucked under maples and oaks on a quiet street across from Grandview grade and high schools. The Elliots lived next door on the south, and shared homemade jelly that was harvested from the grape arbor that filled their back yard. The Friaglias, an aging immigrant Italian couple, lived next door to the north. We knew all the neighbors for houses in all directions, north, south, and backyard neighbors to the west. The postwar years in that neighborhood must have been the inspiration for many of Norman Rockwell's Saturday Evening Post covers. It felt comfortable, peaceful.

The thing I remember best from 1281 was the dinner table. After years of Depression scraps, followed by years of GI mess eaten off cold tin plates, I had fallen into a garden spot, literally. Mickey had a garden out back and he prided himself on his tomatoes. I remember one plant that must have been eight feet tall. Grampa Albert and George had a huge garden and every Sunday visit ended with a trunkful of whatever was harvested. And the Ohio State University Ag School gardens were only a few blocks north, so during growing season we ate like kings.

The dinner table was crowded and lively. Supper was almost always early. Mickey would arrive home from work like clockwork at five twenty-five, and Margaret would have the food ready shortly thereafter. We knew to be on time. My favorites were her veal Marengo, her spaghetti con maiale, her fried green peppers, and when the gods smiled, one of Aunt Rose's blueberry pies.

I established a reputation at that table as the eater of last resort. Anything left on any plate was considered fair game, and I always spoke first. My ploy....I'd eat quickly, creating the impression that I still had room left. Then I'd cast my eyes left and right, looking for any sign of hesitation....a fork set down, a slight push back from the table, even a wriggle that could indicate restlessness.

"You gonna finish that?" I'd get out there before anyone else, usually Joe, had a chance to speak for what might turn out to be an available morsel. I took no umbrage if my interest was rebuked. More often than not, I was able to snap up all available leftovers. I'd never eaten like that in my life.

1281 was chaotic, full of life if one wanted to bestow a kinder appellation. Stephen and John could create more mayhem than the grappling hordes of Arab youth that scavenged any discard from our Algerian camps. They were everywhere, into everything. They ran through the house chasing each until it about drove me insane. They tackled each other. They wrestled each other. They yelled at each other. An additional level of chaos attended the arrival of baby Michael, a beautiful but noisy new roommate. There was no space in the dining room for his crib, so he joined Joe and me in our multi-generational dorm. That was too much ankle-level activity for me. I tried to drown it out by turning up the opera on the radio or phonograph. That soothed me as much as it could, but it was all too much hubbub. I needed to read. I needed to write. I needed to study. That's where my second home came in.

That home was University Hall, site of the Classics Department on the Ohio State campus. If I wanted quiet, I could find it in any of a number of libraries or secluded nooks. If I wanted stimulation, I had my classmates or my wonderful teachers and advisors. I was, for the second time in my life, in my element. And this time no bishop could put an end to it. I was my own master.

Those were the salad days. The Depression was over; the war was over. My future lay in front of me, and surrounded by like-minded folk, it looked glorious. We read the Classics. We attended concerts. We discussed philosophy. We opined on the events shaping Europe under the Marshall plan. We argued politics where I was a stout defender of FDR's vision of a more sharing society. I loved harvesting the wisdom of the Classics and weaving them into visions of how our country could reshape the world. It was then that I knew my destiny, to carry that ageless wisdom to a new generation of hungry minds. I would become the teacher, the Magister. Imbued with a new passion, I raced through the curriculum, completing my undergraduate work in June of 1946, and my Masters, with honors I might add, a year later. I was ready to meet the world. My chosen field, Latin and the Classics, gave me a competitive advantage in the hiring process. I was the only graduate available, and I quickly landed a job in Cincinnati, home, I might add, of the zoo opera and an outstanding symphony. I shed my earlier personas, Crusher the Speedy Fullback and Sgt. Stefano, both alien to my nature, and donned the mantle of Mr. Stefano, Latin and Classics teacher.

Mary

Greenhills, a village north of Cincinnati, was one of the original planned greenbelt communities, a low-income government subsidized housing development. Most of the homes were built in a European townhome style. Our house was one of the few completely separate houses, with our own trees and a lawn. In back of the house was a long hill. All the grounds were free for anyone's use, but privacy was respected in close proximity of the homes. We cut our own grass but in the spring a government mower would cut the hill in back. Our house was located in a large circle of dwellings with an expansive green area in the center. All the children in the neighborhood would gather there to play made-up games.....kick the can, hide and seek, capture the flag. It was a very comfortable place.

There were no department stores in Greenhills, just grocery stores. Twice a year we sent for the Sears and Roebuck catalog and we did all our shopping from that. We would mail in an order and wait anxiously for the big cardboard carton to arrive. It was like Christmas morning when that parcel was delivered.

About a mile from our house was a deserted farm house with a small lake that froze over in the winter. Our family often hiked to that pond to go ice skating. During the time the lake was frozen, the park rangers would build a huge bonfire and put big logs around it for the skaters to sit on and warm themselves. Warm skaters. Warm memories.

About a mile away from the house there was a large swimming pool open free to the public. The water always seemed to be the right temperature. We walked through a shady woods on a wide blacktop path to get to the swimming pool. I remember those walks with my mother. They were our closest times. She had grown up in such a simpler age. Her father pulled her out of high school after less than a year there. He needed help running his office. He paid my mother fifteen dollars a week, then extracted half of that back to pay for her room and board. I learned all this on those walks. We also had our mother-daughter talks on that path. My mother had led such a sheltered life as a young woman. She confessed to me one day that she had originally thought that she could get pregnant by kissing a boy after dark. Maybe my father didn't want his right-hand girl to do anything that would interfere with her work.

I didn't know it then, but now I can put the right name on it... that my parents' marriage was an unhappy one. My mother, who had never dated a soul before marrying my father, graduated from a domineering father to a dominating husband. She never had a chance to grow into who she was. So we'd walk and we'd talk, and occasionally she'd smile or laugh, but mostly she reared children and kept quiet.

That all changed the day Fred moved into our house. Here's how that happened. Greenhills was, as I said, a planned community. But one thing the plan didn't take into account was how to house teachers in the community's school. So like a scene out of the 1860's Great Plains states, the school asked parents who had been assigned one of the three bedroom houses to provide a room for one of the single teachers. We got Fred.

I don't know what my mother thought of this development. My father, who was often and regularly absent at his work, probably appreciated the small check he pocketed each month to cover Fred's room and board. Had he known of Fred's prodigious appetite, he might have held out for a more generous payment. We kids thought it a great honor to have one of our school's teachers as our roommate.

Fred moved in with what we would come to know as his usual great fanfare. He solicited us to help him carry his belongings to his room at the top of the stairs. Fred carried his own phonograph into his room. We didn't have a phonograph in our house at that time and we were dumbstruck. Each of us kids helped carry a stack of 78 rpm records, all operas and symphonies. Whatever my mother might have thought before eyeing those possessions, she was now intrigued and excited about our new guest. She hadn't had much in the way of intellectual stimulation in her life, and she was hungry for it. Fred was a wellspring of culture, intelligence and company. Her heart rate perked up.

Here are the things I remember most about Fred. He was a voracious eater. He'd be the first one at the table, and the last one to leave. There was never a scrap left to toss in the garbage because he'd clinically cleaned each plate. He was also good for an occasional ice cream treat. He might take one of us kids out for a cone, or he might bring home a hand-packed half-gallon on special days, like birthdays or holidays. Dad never did that.

Fred was also an exuberant sharer of things he found exciting, and by that I mainly mean opera and classical music. The kids were less than excited by that quality, but mother loved it. Fred, if he knew she was within hearing distance, would leave his bedroom door open. Mother, if she had the time, would sit on the stairs and listen. If she was busy, she could still hear it throughout the house. Unless of course father was home, in which case Fred showed great discretion and kept his door closed and the volume down.

And Fred would join us on our walks. He seemed to know about everything, and lacked any sense that we might not be too interested in the topic of the day. Nice thing about having a conversation with Fred....you didn't have to do anything but listen. Fred would instruct on the taxonomy of the plants or animals that we encountered. That would trigger a mental connection to a poem in the storehouse that was his mind, and he would recite Longfellow or Shakespeare or whatever poet occurred to him. Mother was in awe. I'd try to walk ahead.

Eventually the common interests of music and poetry and love of nature formed a bond between my mother and Fred and they fell in love. Their relationship stayed platonic, except for one evening when father was not at home and Fred called mother into the kitchen to look out the window at the full moon. That was the one time they kissed. It wasn't long after that that Fred, at the dinner table, made an announcement that shattered my mother.

"I've been hired to teach the soldiers in Japan, and I'll be leaving at the end of the school year."

It was a matter of fact statement to Fred.

It was as if Fred had announced a death in the family to my mother.

Fred

I went to Greenhills to teach. It turned out to be the beginning of a new phase of my learning, not about the Classics but about life.

Greenhills was built in the 1930s as a greenbelt community, set miles north of Cincinnati. It was an island of government optimism about how people could live a neighborly, village life. I don't think they intended one of the consequences of their planning. They forgot about single people. Either that or they were trying to replicate prairie life of a century earlier. The result was that my only accommodation option was living with a family. My whole life I'd been living in a communal environment: in a room shared by me and my brothers in Wilmington; in the dormitory in Nazareth with dozens of boys; in army barracks or camps; or in Margaret and Mickey's house, one of nine people in a one-bathroom house. I'd been hoping for my own space. But Greenhills hadn't anticipated a young, bachelor teacher.

So I became the star boarder in the Toren household. I arrived a few days before classes were to start and enlisted Mary and Gary, two of the children, to help me unload my meager possessions. One load consisted of my civilian clothes and two boxes of books. On the second trip up the stairs, I carried my most prized possession, a portable GE phonograph. Mary and Gary carried stacks of my classical music collection. At the urging of their mother Ruth I was broadcasting to the four corners of the house within minutes. Mary and Gary quickly disappeared, but Ruth stayed....for what turned out to be for the rest of her life.

As we walked the paths through the greenbelt surrounding Greenhills, which we did for endless hours, I told her of the path that had led me from Wilmington to Greenhills, and she revealed, although haltingly and with my constant encouragement, the story of a young woman who had led a captive life, first by her father and then by her husband. I couldn't help but feel protective of her, and I wanted to share with her all the learning and wonders that the world had to offer. As you might guess, it was new territory for both of us, and we wandered and stumbled into love. It was magic. And it was complicated.

I knew she was unhappy in her marriage. I knew she was trapped in a situation where she could not grow. I cared deeply about her. And I knew it could lead to sin, a step that I was incapable of taking. If I'd stayed close, I don't know if I could have stayed true to my beliefs, or maybe I should say 'the church's beliefs.' So, still trapped in my youthful and untested principles, I fled for safety.

When I heeded the dictum to avoid the 'near occasion of sin,' I took it to the extremes. I was going to avoid even the 'distant occasion of sin.'

Next stop, a US Army base in Japan. I looked hard for an escape route and found an ad for an English teacher for US troops in Japan. Not too many people were that interested in returning to the country of our former enemy, so I was quickly hired and dispatched. I imagined my sacrifice akin to that of a saint who gave up personal desires in service to the Lord, not say on the order of a martyr like St. Stephen or St. Valentine, but at least deserving of minor recognition. After all, I was giving up the most important relationship of my life. I imagined substantial credit on the pages of St. Peter's Good Book.

I did allow myself to write Ruth. At first it was an almost daily ritual. Eventually guilt would overwhelm me and I'd make myself stop for a while. Then the hunger for some contact with her would overtake me, and I'd again allow myself the simple pleasure of correspondence. She would always answer me.

It was a time of great personal struggle for me. There was little opportunity on that base for entertainment or intellectual exchange, so I turned in on myself, questioning how I'd formed my values. It was obvious when I thought about it that I really hadn't formed any of my moral foundation. I'd been handed the entire score, dawn to dusk, week to week, table to bed, covering every facet of my life, by the church. That was an unsettling recognition. I started exploring the boundaries of the box I'd been living in, first allowing myself the freedom to question all authority, and later experiencing the exhilaration of applying that independence to something more tangible than thought.

I went into the nearest town one evening, intent on pushing the limits of my prison. I headed straight for a geisha house where one of my students told me I could find companionship. I knew he meant physical contact which was both intriguing and frightening at the same moment. I was more than a bit nervous at the prospect as I stood outside the opaque paneled door of the house, but the loneliness provided the courage to push me across that threshold. I was served tea and a small pastry and was soon introduced to the most beautiful woman I'd ever met. She was young, slender, a classic Oriental face, dressed in the traditional Japanese gown. She ushered me to a room where we could relax and visit. This was new territory for me and I nervously I began to question her...where had she been during the war? what was it like when her country was attacked by our bombers? what were her plans for the future? She seemed pleased by my interest and sat back a short distance from me and answered each question thoughtfully and in great detail. She seemed to be a very cultured woman, and more confident than I would have expected for someone of such a young age. We talked until the hostess interrupted us to tell her that my time was up. Mizuki, that was her name, told me that I was the most interesting and sensitive man that she had ever met, that she hoped she would see me again. I'm no fool. I know that was probably a line she told everyone who visited her. But it opened a door for me that allowed questions, explorations, options. The thought of freedom was coursing through my veins, and I was never quite the same again.

Mary

The years that Fred was teaching in Japan were terribly hard for my mother. She'd been introduced to a way of relating that she'd never experienced before. She'd grown dependent on Fred to feed these new freedoms, and was literally starving when he was gone. His letters were the closest thing she had to a lifeline, and she'd await the daily arrival of the postman. I could tell if he'd written by the angle of her shoulders as she inspected the daily harvest from the mailbox, upright if there was a letter from Fred, sagging if not. There were times that Fred would stop writing and those were the hardest. My mother couldn't understand why her best friend would go weeks without a word. I'd find her crying in the kitchen, a stack of meaningless mail on the table.

I felt sorry for the both of them..... for my mother who had tasted nurturing and support for the first time in her life, and who now was thousands of miles from its source.

I felt sorry for Fred too. He was such an innocent, toiling in an intellectual wasteland when I knew he'd rather be teaching in Greenhills. One incident stands out in my memory that captures their suffering better than any words I could conscript for the task.

One day I found mother sobbing uncontrollably in the kitchen. There was a letter crumpled at her feet on the kitchen floor. I picked it up and could tell immediately from the stationery and hand that it was a letter from Fred. Mother's tears begged the question, "Mother, what's wrong?"

She just nodded to the discarded note. I picked it up and read.

Fred, writing as if it were a college English paper, described a visit he'd made to a Japanese geisha house. He waxed poetic on the beauty of his hostess. He described in excruciating detail the thrill he'd experienced with this woman. Inspired by her claims that he was the most exciting man she'd ever met, Fred had returned to the house the next evening, bearing gifts of flowers, candy and perfume.

"I'm here to see Mizuki," he'd informed the hostess.

"She's with someone right now," he was brutally informed, "but I'm sure she'd be glad to see you if you can come back in a few hours."

Fred was devastated. He'd imagined her sitting demurely on her couch, awaiting Fred's return and her rescue into the world that only Fred could open.

And he told this tale, in antiseptic and clinical terms, to the one woman in the world who truly did love him. Fred was a gentle soul and I know he'd never do anything to intentionally hurt my mother, but sometimes he was as clueless as a newborn lamb.

As a footnote to that story, I will tell you that Fred, when he departed to Japan, had left behind his portable phonograph and record collection for my mother to enjoy. My mother was never again able to look at the cover of his copy of "Madame Butterfly," adorned by a photo of Cio-Cio-San, known as Madame Butterfly, or to play that reminder of Fred breaking her heart.

<u>Fred</u>

I had a lot of time to think while I was teaching in Japan. There wasn't much else to do. Thinking led to an almost feverish inquiry into the Catholic faith. I read everything I could get my hands on, which given my isolation in a hard-sided tent on a Japanese plain, was somewhat limited. I began to understand my religion more on an intellectual basis than on blind acceptance. Things were jettisoned that blind acceptance had, well, accepted

Here's a little of the path I traveled and where I ended up: Fred Stefano was stationed in a remote part of the world, remote from where he wanted to be, near Ruth, and what he wanted to be doing, exposing bright students to the wisdom of the Classics. Why?. . . . because of guilt over loving someone and wanting to be near her. It got very basic with me, starting with working out a definition of what religion was. Here's what I came up with . . . I actually wrote it down .... *Religion is a system that guides its proponents in their relationship with the creator, and ultimately with the truths and values that flow from Him.* I'd have preferred a non-gender pronoun for 'Him,' but I didn't like 'it' and was more focused at that point on the bigger picture. Ultimately I compared my intentions, which I defined as service to others, with what I thought a loving God would bless. I concluded that the Church was derailing me from a righteous path. I wasn't ready to abandon the Church, but I was now ready to negotiate my relationship with it.

My contract with the US Army was for two years, and on the day it expired I was on a plane, a TWA Constellation, back to the United States. I had secured a position teaching Latin in the high school in Mechanicsburg, Ohio. With no moral anxiety at all, I was back where I wanted to be, doing what I wanted to be doing.

The relationship with Ruth was resumed, albeit on a platonic basis. When we were able to see each other, we shared the walks, the talks, our love of music and nature, trips to the opera, but we kept our relationship chaste. Her husband, who paid little attention to Ruth, felt no threat from a harmless, poetry-quoting Latin teacher. Things were comfortable during those few years. Fate decided to throw a pop quiz at us when the school system in Mechanicsburg, infected by the fad du jour, 'progressive education,' decided to drop Latin from their curriculum. I never was given the chance to make a presentation to the school board on the values of the Classics. They were focused on preparing their students for jobs, not life. I was unable to secure a position teaching Latin any closer than Waukegan, Illinois.

That distance posed a problem. Neither of us had the resources to permit frequent travel to see each other. The same was true for phone calls which we also couldn't afford. Something needed to give.

I don't remember this part, but Ruth seemed to have it vividly in her store. Apparently I started making noises about needing to find a girlfriend if I was ever going to get married and start a family. I had never considered that Ruth might someday be available. She had. It wasn't long after that that one of her letters carried a message that led to the happiest days of my life. Hers too. She had filed for divorce and was packing for a move to Waukegan, that if a marriage proposal was an option. I couldn't believe it . . . Ruth and me married? I couldn't imagine my good fortune. I told her I'd drive down to Cincinnati to pick her up as soon as she was packed.

I hadn't stopped to consider that the Church might not permit us the sacrament of marriage.

In fact it did not. "There is no possibility that I or any other priest can marry you in the Catholic Church. Ruth is divorced and that's that," Father Rooney declared.

I tried to argue, but he ended the conversation with, "No, Fred. And that's the final word."

I'd reached another milestone in my relationship with the Church. Father Rooney's words were a disappointment, not a barrier. We knew that our relationship could thrive without the Church, but that we could not without each other. The Church again took a back seat to life. We'd participate as much as we'd be permitted, but we instituted our own set of sacraments based on nature and music and our own company. We could both live with that.

Ruth and I shared thirty-five years of marriage, 'without benefit of sacrament,' as the saying goes. We moved to California when the Waukegan schools terminated the Latin program, again under the sway of that university-generated foolishness, 'progressive education,' and I was assigned to teach history to a class of 'under-achieving' students. I have never been known for my patience, and the underachievers surpassed my tolerance levels immediately. Mary, Ruth's daughter and a dazzling young woman, had gotten married and moved to California. We followed along shortly after and took up temporary residence in Mary's new home.

It wasn't easy finding a teaching job there. Ruth taught piano lessons to bring in some income. I was eventually hired to teach Latin in Watsonville and although we had very little money, we were rich beyond measure. Ruth's children all took me in as one of their own, and my concerns about starting a family were all of a sudden dissolved. I had all the family I would ever need. Those were the happiest days of my life, the halcyon days.

Mary

In 1958 the winds of change were blowing through the country. The Dodgers and Giants broke some hearts and thrilled others when they bolted their old bonds and headed west. On a somewhat smaller scale, our family followed suit. We scattered from Cincinnati and fled toward happier lives.

My mother, ending years of an unhappy marriage, divorced my father, married Fred and joined him in Waukegan. Fred, who had earlier come *through* our lives, the star boarder in our Greenhills home, now came *into* our lives. He became our new father, the man who would introduce years of hilarity into the family lore.

Fred was full of energy, and it spilled out onto everyone around him. Fred bounced through life, enjoying everything within sight, sound or smell, and shared that enthusiasm with us, whether we were interested or not. I don't know if Fred knew how to love in the Hollywood sense. I don't think he ever said, "I love you." He wasn't like a puppy dog that you could embrace or hold on your lap. He was more like a presence that exuded joy, reflecting all those sights, sounds, smells that delighted him. You couldn't stop it. You couldn't turn down the volume. We learned to just let him shine. And the warmth spread.

And Fred was a story waiting to happen. I'm sure that is why these stories are being told now. They're too good to let fade. And they are funny. And a part of the fun was Fred listening to the stories being told about himself, and his explosion of laughter at his own antics. There was no embarrassment in the man. He loved being the star of his own life.

Where to start? We could start small. When my mother and Fred first moved to California, they lived with me while they were getting established. Soon they bought a home shaded in the redwoods but that proved to be too damp for my mother's allergies. They needed new surroundings. Gary agreed to build them a home in Bonny Doon, and while it was under construction, they sold their home and moved into a tiny motel room on the beach at Rio Del Mar. I'll never forget the Christmas we celebrated there. The unit was too small for a full-sized Christmas tree, so they purchased a tiny artificial tree and placed it on a slatted table by the window. Presents were strewn about it and beneath it on the floor. When Christmas morn dawned California-clear, we sat around the tree waiting for Santa, aka Fred, to distribute the presents. First one then the next discovered that our presents were soaking wet. How could that be? As Elaine said on a Seinfeld episode, "Oh, it be!" Fred had conscientiously watered the tiny tree....you get the picture: water, slatted table, soaked presents. We howled, not in disappointment but in delight.

Then there was the time Fred and mother drove to the pharmacy to pick up a prescription. Fred couldn't find a legal parking place, so he pulled to the curb, left mother in the car lest the police arrive and try to write a ticket, and Fred raced inside, quickly retrieved the medicine, and raced back to the car. He jumped in, turned on the ignition, and was met with a banshee scream. The woman next to him was yelling at the top of her lungs while fumbling through her purse for her Mace. Fred was quick to realize that he'd hopped into the wrong car. Without so much as apology, he bolted to his own car and sped off before 'the cops arrived.' Vintage Fred.

Fred was hapless, a certified klutz. I think it was because his mind was not on the step in front of him, not on the world his body was in, but was off on a merry adventure to places imagined or remembered. Usually it was harmless enough. We could all survive water-soaked Christmas presents. But sometimes it could have had a less humorous ending. As in the time Gary ran out of gas on Highway 1, California's famed coastal highway. He called Fred who charged to the rescue, picked up Gary and drove him to a nearby service station. Gary drove

Fred's car back to the stalled vehicle when Fred admitted he didn't remember where that was. A five gallon can of gas was dumped into Gary's empty tank. Gary thanked Fred and told him he'd meet him back at the house. So far, so good.

Here's where things went wrong. Fred started his car, put the gear shift lever into reverse, and hit the gas. Nothing. Fred was perplexed. This had never happened before. You hit the gas, the car goes. But not this time. A brief inspection and logical analysis of the situation led to the discovery that Gary had applied the emergency brake. Fred had never once used the emergency brake, but had the notion that it was somewhere 'down there.' He reached under the dash, found nothing familiar, so he opened the car door and got out to inspect the underside of the dash to see where the controls might be. He quickly spotted and identified the hand brake, figured out how it worked, and released it . . . while kneeling on the ground, beside and partially under the car. Now the car did what it was supposed to do. It went backward. Fred instinctively grabbed the steering wheel and hung on for dear life as the car backed out across the parking lot and toward US Highway 1 traffic, headed for the far side of the pavement and a 200 foot drop-off to the Pacific below. Fortunately for Fred, two young men in a pickup truck spotted his dilemma, jumped out of their truck, raced to Fred's rescue, leapt into the runaway vehicle and turned off the ignition before Fred plunged to a watery grave.

I suppose that many of us, had we experienced such a trauma, might have shared the story with our loved ones. Fred certainly did. And more than loved ones. More like Known Ones. Church folks. Senior Center bridge partners. Almost anyone who would listen.

The usual response, after the shock and horror subsided, was, "Fred, were you seriously hurt?"

To which Fred invariably replied, "I scraped a basketball-sized patch of skin off my butt" as he dropped his trousers and mooned the unsuspecting and unprepared audience. Neither the blunder nor the bare ass embarrassed the man. He was there to share his life, arse, warts and all as the saying goes.

Fred and my mother had an idyllic marriage. They were interested in the same things: music, particularly opera and the classic symphonies, the arts, nature. They were completely devoted to each other. And for a long while our family had a good run in the "Ozzie and Harriet mode....birthday parties, holiday dinners, all around good times.

Both mother and Fred took their religion seriously and I know they were disappointed by the Church's failure to recognize their marriage. I remember the day that mother called me, her joy broadcast out of her voice.

"Guess what." I could tell it was a good thing.

"Father Siro said that we can receive the sacraments. That we can participate fully in all the Church's services."

I knew how much that meant, both to her and to Fred. "Mother, that is wonderful news" I was able to get out before,

"There's more. Father Siro invited Fred to become a Lector and to read the gospel at Sunday mass. I've never seen him this happy. He's literally on cloud nine."

Fred was back in the fold, back in a place that was important to him. We'd had discussions over the years about religion, and Fred had explained his negotiated relationship with the Church, but I could tell that was an intellectual negotiation, not an emotional one. Now the two components of Fred's personality were free to inhabit the same body. We drove down the first Sunday Fred was scheduled to read. The Church calls the bible the 'good news' of God's love. Fred's voice did that 'good news' proud. He boomed it. He lilted it. He inflected it. He sang it. A less confident priest might have felt outshone by Fred's theatrics. Fr. Siro just beamed at Fred's rebirth.

The salad days didn't last forever. The Watsonville schools decided to drop Latin, the third time that Fred had been cut adrift by a school system that failed to share his devotion to the Classics. He was heartsick. He earned certification as a librarian and continued to be employed, but not overjoyed.

"I'm nothing but a damn 'shusher,'" he characterized his forced transition from educator to disciplinarian.

Mother's heart eventually began to wear out and that led to an increasing dementia. Mother needed continual care and supervision. My brother Wally was living with Gary at that time and so was nearby. He'd come to the house at 8 each morning to tend to mother while Fred took care of town chores. Fred would relieve Wally in the afternoon and look after her until the next morning.

Mother's dementia led to a difficult time for Fred. She began to grow distant from him, imagining one time that he was off running with 'his whore.'

Another time she whispered to me, "Fred has moved me into this different house. And you can't believe it. They have the exact same furniture as we do. You've got to take me home." There was no arguing with mother. She was absolutely convinced of Fred's duplicity. So I put her in her wheelchair, walked out the front door and down the block, turned around and wheeled her home to "Oh thank you. Thank you."

Fred took it all in stride. He really was a saint in those times, never wavering in his concern and his love for her. "She can't help it," he'd try to console us.

Mother passed away, her heart failing her for the last time. I think that was the low point in Fred's life. As usual, he found a way to look at it that buoyed him.

"She's gone on to heaven. I'll catch up with her soon."

Lisa and I kept a closer eye on Fred after that. We were worried that he'd lose his enthusiasm for life. We could have relaxed. Fred was still Fred, enjoying his role as senior member of the family. He never missed one of David's soccer games, although his solidarity came with a price.

"I'll be over to pick you up at 2," Lisa phoned him.

"Before you come, I want you to know that I have conditions."

"Conditions?' Lisa couldn't have known where he might be going with that. She remembers hoping that it didn't refer to his unpredictable bowels.

"No more tepid water. I want juice, cold juice. I want snacks. I want nuts. Not like last time. Okay?"

Lisa thought back to the previous Saturday's game and the uninspiring supplies she'd brought along, one plastic container of tap water. "I'll bring some good snacks, Fred. Don't worry."

Months passed and Lisa thought that Fred seemed lonely. A friend of hers mentioned that she too knew a lonely old person. The two of them hatched a scheme to get them together. Fred at first was hesitant. "I'm perfectly happy by myself," he protested. But he eventually agreed to a date. That led to more dates, and in due course to his marriage to Denise.

If we could be offered a do-over on that one, we might rethink it. If 'funny' was our goal, we'd get a decent grade on that score. In the long run I'm not sure we did either of them any favors.

Steve

Here's a brief confessional, a report on an inglorious chapter in the Fred stories. It's more about me than about Fred. It's an admission that it took me a long time to understand Fred or properly value him. I'm ashamed of this episode, but it's part of the record and needs its place in the family story.

The occasion was brother Mark's fiftieth birthday. Debbie arranged a surprise birthday party and the family flew in from all points on the map. We arrived at San Francesco International Airport, rented vehicles and headed south on the coast highway, our destination a motel in Pacific Grove. Our path took us through Santa Cruz, the highway but a few blocks from Fred's residence. We opted not to stop on our way down, our focus on the celebration ahead. That and the fact that Fred was no fun, not our kind of guy, hard to be around. He was loud and very talkative and animated and, well, just plain no fun to be around.

We stopped a few miles south in Monterey for lunch at a wharf-side diner. Our view to the north was the expanse of Monterey Bay. As the fish and chips were served, the topic of "What should we do about Fred?" came up. There were no votes for "Maybe we should invite him, or at least go see him." We'd all grown up around Fred's temper and verbal overachievement, and none of us had the inclination to voluntarily subject ourselves to that punishment. Michael, casting eyes about for any familiar faces, unlikely this far from home, suggested that maybe we shouldn't use Fred's actual name in these deliberations lest someone who knew him might overhear.

The story turns a bit funny at this point. Jan, who had been to the hair stylist the day before leaving, offered this story and suggestion:

"While I was in the chair yesterday, one of the gray-haired ladies at the shop was describing to the others present that she had a new liaison at the retirement home, not yet a blossoming love affair but at least someone to get interested in. Inquisitive minds had to know, 'What's his name?'"

Favoring discretion over braggadocio, she invented, "Let's just call him Kenneth."

Well, as you might have guessed at this juncture, future reference to Fred was now, and for years into the future, under the nom de guise (there is such a phrase, isn't there? If not, you catch my drift) of Kenneth. For a very long time none of us could utter the word 'Kenneth' without an accompanying chortle. 'Weak game' as my old friend Shriver would have judged it. And weak game it was. It took us all a while to grow out of that childishness and reset our attitude toward our uncle.

The unkindness had little toxic impact on the birthday proceedings, although the golfing gods may have been responsible for a bit of chastisement when they sent cold Pacific showers down upon our eagerly anticipated golf match. We survived, but shivered a lot.

The celebrations lasted until Sunday when we hit the road to catch our planes out of San Francisco. I remember it was the weekend of the NFL playoffs, and planeloads of Cheeseheads were invading the airport to cheer on their beloved Packers. Mike and Kathy were riding with us, and Michael, who was probably closest to Freddie, remarked that we were about to be safe in our stealthy avoidance of Fred, aka Kenneth.

"We just passed the turnoff to Fred's house at that last intersection. Fred's church is less than a mile further up this road. The only chance we'd have to encounter him would be in the next few hundred feet. We're safe now."

If this were a movie plot, the next scene would be implausible, improbable, unbelievable. The very next car passing us going the other way was driven by an old man, a man seated so low that he was peering fixedly and straight ahead between the top rim of the steering wheel and the dashboard, a man wearing his characteristic and unmistakable Scottish tam, a man who was none other than.....Kenneth.

Jan screamed,"It's him!" Michael, Kathy and Jan instinctively ducked in their seats. I had my eyes fixed for a moment on the other driver and could tell he'd never taken his eyes off the road "It's all clear. You can come up now. He didn't see us. And it was him."

We marveled at the coincidence. Years later, now that he's gone, we'd all take back that slight, that blight on our records, all reference to Kenneth, and we'd have had our eccentric uncle join in the celebration. Maybe the golf gods would issue us a do-over on that miserable round of golf.

JB.... *My brother is being too hard on himself. Fred was a load. He terrorized us as kids, our only escape from his Italian temper and swiftly wielded hair brush/paddle was our ability to outrun and out-maneuver him as we tore up the stairs to the safety of the bathroom door's blessed lock.*

And talk? The man had no limit. Time of day? Didn't matter. Subject matter? Anything was fair game. His most frequent topic was "the bastard politicians," usually a Republican. George W. Bush drove Fred to apoplexy.

Somehow Fred thought me an interested listener and I was the recipient of many an evening or late night phone call. I learned to cope. I hated to be disrespectful but there were few nights when I didn't have many miles to travel before I slept. My coping mechanism...I'd listen while Fred launched his tirade, wait until I felt comfortable that he was on a roll, then I'd set the phone down, go make myself a sandwich or uncap a bottle of beer, and eventually return to the phone, Fred never the wiser that I'd been momentarily absent. Saved me valuable time and met Fred's need to share.

Julie

Fred had graduated from the university and moved from our house before I was born, so I hadn't known him at an early age. But later in life, when he and Ruth had moved to California, and when I had moved there, I developed a wonderful relationship with the two of them. To be more accurate, I became very close to Ruth who saw me as a young woman far from home and needing some mothering. I spent many a pleasant day in their home in the redwoods, Ruth fetching me tea, wrapping me in a blanket if the coast was delivering one of its misty chills, and treating me like a princess. The tea was comforting and warming, but her attention was what I valued most. She spent time with me, asked me questions, listened to my answers. She became like a second mother to me. Fred was always around, giving off nervous energy but rarely participating in the conversations. He'd retreat to his study where the sounds of some symphony would provide background music to the rest of the house. I remember my brothers describing the Fred Era, when opera invaded our Grandview home. They seemed to tolerate Fred but didn't have a close relationship with him the way they did with my father's brothers.

Eventually I moved north to Portland so my visits became less frequent. I'd hear from Mary tales of Ruth's illnesses and gradual decline into dementia. My geriatric social worker skills could have been of value to her. My adopted daughter concern could have provided some comfort. I felt guilty, a trait ingrained by my Catholic school upbringing, that I couldn't be there for Ruth like she had been there for me.

The call came from Mary one morning. Ruth had passed away in her sleep. I think we all felt, besides our sense of loss, a feeling of relief. She'd been freed from the mental torment that had made her last months a trial for her and all around her. At the funeral Fred was surrounded by his family: Mary, Gary, their children and grandchildren. He appeared to be in good hands. But weeks later I got a call from Fred.

"Julie, it's me. Your Uncle Fred" . . . as if I could ever fail to recognize that voice. He was calling to see how I was doing.

"I know Ruth was very dear to you. I was concerned about you."
I remember thinking at that moment . . . *Fred, you were paying attention all those times you absented yourself. You were giving us space.*

That call opened up a new chapter, maybe Chapter One, in my relationship with Fred. He'd call often, many times late at night, the pretext being concern for how I was dealing with the loss of Ruth. My professional life is spent identifying signs of depression. Fred was a textbook case:

He was sad, tearful. I could tell he was losing interest in the things that had always brought him pleasure. He talked about difficulty sleeping. He talked about losing interest in food, a sure sign something was wrong given his lifelong love affair with things edible. He was agitated (check); fatigued (check); guilty at Ruth's decline (check); had trouble concentrating (check). When I say textbook, I'm being literal. He earned a checkmark in every box on my list. And he often talked about death. I was worried that he was contemplating suicide.

I called Mary. I should have known. They were on top of it, as much as they could be from outside his skin. They saw Fred every day. They lured him out to the grandkids sporting events. They had him to Sunday dinner. They were being the family that Fred needed. It was as much as anyone could do.

Michael

I could kick myself for not videotaping the wedding. I should have known it would be one for the ages. I'd had a front row seat to all the prenuptial episodes. Why would the culmination of years of maneuvering be any less histrionic or hysterical than the preceding scenes that played out to my audience?

Fred had gotten into the habit of calling on a regular basis to report the unfolding of his relationship with Denise. I suspect I drew the winning hand because I was geographically the closest, and therefore the least costly long distance call. I can think of no other reason for my election as confessor-in-chief. Whatever the selection criteria, I was the Chosen One, the receiver of unlimited insights into a blossoming quasi-romance. I say "quasi" because it was only half a romance. Denise was determined to ensnare Fred. Fred was equally motivated to maintain his status as a free man. After the early calls, I would not have known where to place my bets. Both of them held firm and irreconcilable positions. But I would soon learn whose hand held all the aces.

"Michael, this is your Uncle Fred," he announced late one evening. I hadn't invested in Caller ID at that time, but had I, it might have saved me many painful cases of Telephone Ear, an unofficial but widely understood malady. But I hadn't the needed warning, so I was enlisted into the first of many lengthy listening sessions. I would say 'conversations,' but it doesn't really count as one if I didn't get a chance to actually say anything. Fred had made the call; it was his dime; and he wasn't going to waste toll charges on anything I might have had to say.

Turns out Mary's son's wife had a friend, a single lady, who wanted to meet Fred, go out on a date.

"I'm too old to date," Fred argued. "Plus why would I want to date anyway? I'm almost eighty years old."

I was starting to formulate a list of why he might want to date, but it turned out to be a rhetorical question and Fred was off to the races.

He enumerated a litany of all the activities that filled his life....thrice-weekly bridge games at the Senior Center; daily senior lunches at the aforesaid center, and the interesting conversations (one-sided, likely) that ensued; his Sunday ritual of being the lector at Fr. Siro's mass; the delightful visits with Ruth's children, their assorted wives and husbands; the grandchildren and their myriad sports and school activities. No sir, his life was full and he had no intention of getting into any new relationship.

Chalk up one for Fred's resolve.

The next call detailed the invite from Denise to spend the weekend at her daughter's house. The call after that revealed some of the tactics of that marital trap.

"She put us in the same bedroom," Fred indignantly reported. "Denise was bound and determined to have sex. First of all, I can't have sex with her. We're not married and it would be a mortal sin. And second, I don't want to have sex. I just don't get all that wiggling and thrashing down there."

I had no trouble interpreting his 'down there' reference.

"So how'd it work out for you?" I was able to insert.

Fred had taken the moment to draw a fresh breath, "I pretended to have a headache," he proudly reported, thinking somehow that he'd pulled off a fast one. I began to formulate the odds in Denise' favor.

89

A new entrant in the Fred Derby was reported in the next phone call. A ninety-one- year-old regular at the Senior Center bridge table had expressed interest in an expanded relationship with Fred. Maybe she was starved for conversation and had spotted the mother lode of Fred's verbal offerings. She apparently hadn't mentioned sex as of yet, but the way things were going I didn't figure it was off the table for long. I began wondering if Hollywood wasn't missing an entire market segment, love stories and porno-warm-up films for the Plus 90 set. Fred dismissed the newest player, discounting her casual mention of a substantial retirement nest egg with "She can't count points. She doesn't bid Goren. She can't remember which cards have been played. She drives me crazy."

Her competition written off, Denise apparently took her game up a notch after Fred had made it clear that he was a 'free spirit" and had no intention of getting married. She stopped calling him; refused to answer his calls; and failed to drive him to church the following Sunday. Four aces to Fred's ten high. They went shopping for a wedding ring the following weekend.

His ride to church now secured, Fred resumed life as usual and Denise began the process of getting her previous marriage annulled, a pre-condition set by the evasive target of her affections. The dispensation proved no easy task and months passed with Fred holding tightly to his "Get Out of Bed Free" card, the specter of sinfulness protecting his 'down there' assets.

Finally the sacred approbation arrived and wheels that led to the altar were set in motion. The date was set; the church booked; and I was drafted as the Best Man. That's when I should have booked the video team.

The big day arrived, California-sunny. Small issues first. Denise vetoed the tie Fred had chosen and the two of us were sent on a shopping trip with detailed instructions, down to color, width, pattern and fabric, on what Fred's neckwear should be. The mission was accomplished, the side benefit being that it distracted Fred for a good two hours when he would have otherwise been fretting.

He and I arrived at the church an hour early, the better to deal with a serious disappointment. The call had informed Fred that his best buddy, Fr. Siro Dal Dagan, was ill and would not be able to perform the ceremony as planned. A very nice young Jesuit would be filling in. This news unsettled Fred. Father Siro was his best buddy. Fr. Siro had named Fred his finest Lector and had given Fred the pulpit each Sunday for the reading of the gospel. Fr. Siro was the one who had assured Fred that sainthood was a distinct possibility, a claim that I believe Fred might have read more into than Fr. Siro intended. Fr. Siro was the one who had counseled Fred that sex with Denise, after marriage, would not violate any church rules, her divorced status notwithstanding. Fred wanted Fr. Siro, not some 'nice young Jesuit.' Fred aimed to take his measure.

Fr. Healey (not his real name, changed for reasons that will later become evident), the 'nice young Jesuit,' ushered us into his office behind the sacristy. Fred inspected him the way Sherlock Holmes would have devoured clues from the interview of a murder suspect. Things went well enough until Fr. Healey, going over the script for the ceremony came to the "And the woman shall be subservient to the man" part.

Fred interrupted. "We can't say it that way. It's a 50-50 deal, equals on everything. Just leave that part out," he instructed.

The 'nice young Jesuit,' Rome-trained and very confident in his liturgy, was taken aback by Fred's request.

"I can't do that," he replied with a bit of a stiff back. "I'll read it the way it is written."

"But Fr. Siro said we could change those words," Fred argued, his Italian temper injecting an edge into his tone.

"Well, Fr. Siro is not here, and I am, and we'll read the prayers the way God meant them to be read." His tone had an air of finality to it.

But not final to Fred. He'd had about all the authority he could handle from the church, and he wasn't willing to admit Fr. Healey's interpretation of God's will. His face turned red and he exploded, "It's my wedding and we'll do it the way I want it done."

"Not in my church," Fr. Healey held his ground. He looked directly at me. "Get him out of here, NOW!" Now that had an air of finality that both of us could understand. I grabbed Fred's arm, spun him around, and marched him out the door.

"No use arguing with that fellow," I advised Fred.

"It's not over," Fred mumbled as we headed for the waiting room in the fellowship hall. We'd await the appointed hour, noon, with Fred fidgeting and muttering about the unkind turn of events.

At five minutes until noon, Fred and I headed back to the altar. Fr. Healey met us there, the two of them eying each other with what could easily have been interpreted as venomous, acid-laced hostility. Not an auspicious beginning. As we stood at the threshold of the altar, Denise appeared in the church doorway. She was by herself, looking around in apparent search for her attendants. None were in sight. She appeared to be as nervous as Fred, who was giving off enough energy to light a small subdivision. He kept tugging at his sleeve, checking his watch the way a condemned man might devour the ticking clock on the death row wall. No call from the governor was going to save him this time.

At precisely twelve noon, both hands straight up, Fred nodded to Fr. Healey; Fr. Healey nodded to the organist; and the organ boomed out the familiar "Here Comes the Bride." We turned our faces to the church door where Denise, still alone, weighed her options . . . wait for her attendants or succumb to the tradition of the music. Tradition won. She gathered herself, straightened her gown, and marched forward. All eyes were on her as she stepped, stopped, stepped, stopped her way up the aisle. By the time she reached us and took Fred's hand, there was enough unspoken energy between them to light up the whole town.

Minutes later, Denise' son, whose role had been to walk her up the aisle and who had been late in arriving and was in the parking lot putting on and tying his shoe laces, raced through the church door, took the measure of his now irrelevant status, and meekly slid into his front row seat. A minute or so after that a tiny blond five-year-old girl, decked out in frilly finery and carrying a basket of flower petals, repeated the scene, but with no apparent embarrassment at her late arrival. The cast was now assembled, if now beside the point.

The mass unfolded and things appeared to settle down as liturgy trumped angst, the familiar over the unknown, the lull before the storm, which arrived in the form of the earlier debated line.

Fred, familiar with the liturgy, knew the moment was at hand and drilled the 'nice young Jesuit' with a gaze that would have melted uranium. Fr. Healey, backed by two thousand years of papal authority, intoned in his best canonical voice, "And the woman shall be subservient to the man." At which point, Fred, who had been kneeling, jumped up, raised his right arm topped with a rigid, heaven-pointed, index finger and shouted, "I object!!"

The congregation, unaware of the previous dialog between the two, was unprepared for the theater unfolding. All eyes were drawn to the drama, anxious for the next line.

Fr. Healey had to ad lib. Nowhere in his training had he been instructed on how to handle an objection. He resorted to the power of the cloth.

"Shut up and kneel down," he bellowed, hoping the weight of his voice would still the dissent. It didn't. But Denise' strong right arm and her iron grip on Fred's left wrist accomplished what the threat of hell's fires had not. Fred's knees hit the inadequately padded kneeler with a thud heard in the back row. Fr. Healey, emboldened by a success not of his own making, continued.

From the rear of the church a child's voice was heard, "Why are those men shouting, Daddy?" It was Mary's grandson four-year-old Jake. Fr. Healey, now finely tuned to the risk of insurrection, stopped his monolog and stared intently at the source of the insult to his control. And stared with no result. And continued staring until Jake's father, more respectful than confrontational, picked the youngster up and took him outside. Fr. Healey counted it a victory, failing to register that he was now in the estimation of one and all in attendance the much despised and long to be remembered "shithead young Jesuit."

Everyone was ready for this to be over, Fr. Healey included. When he asked, "If there is anyone present who knows why this marriage should not be blessed, speak now or forever hold your peace," peace was held and he was able to bless the marriage and bolt for the sacristy. I put my hand on the envelope that had been destined for the padre's pocket, checking to see that my pocket had not been picked. I could imagine many better uses for the bills inside.

One last scene of that afternoon sticks in my memory. Fred and Denise had rented a stretch limo for ride to the reception hall. The limo had a sun roof. As the vehicle entered the main street of Davenport, Fred stood on the seat, stuck the top half of his body out the opening, and began to wave at the Saturday afternoon crowds. Denise' strong right arm was able to finally jerk him back seatward, but not before a few of the gawkers wondered," Who was that white-haired man? Is the Pope in town?' And not before I was able, from the car behind them, able to shoot a memorable photograph. I even PhotoShopped a halo over his head, an image I hold dear.

Mark....In reviewing my brother's version of events that day, I can only add one glimpse that he has either forgotten or intentionally covered up. After the fall from grace by the "shithead young Jesuit," when all semblance of respect had evaporated, I did observe the Best Man issue what I knew to be a visible if subtle rebuke. The priest was dutifully reading his script:

Happy are you who are poor, for yours is the kingdom of God.

Happy are you who hunger now, for you will be satisfied.

Happy are you who weep now, for you will laugh. And on the through the litany of "Happys"

Brother Michael was bouncing his head up and down and he was doing a little Snoopy dance, to the tune I heard him mutter, "Happy, Happy, Happy."

Reminded me why we all gave up on church a long time ago.

Steve

If I were titling chapters, I'd call this one "Reintroduction to Fred." I have little recollection of any contact with Fred from the time he moved away after graduating from Ohio State. He must have come back to Columbus on occasion and I'm sure I saw him, but I have no memory of that. I've scanned through hundreds of photographs and can only find one where he and I are pictured together. That photo was taken was in California, on brother Michael's back deck, sometime in the early 90s judging by the ages of Amelia and Abby in that picture. I can't remember what we were celebrating on that trip. I have a vague memory that I visited him and Ruth in one of their homes tucked into the California redwoods. I seem to remember the towering trees and the shady nature of the home. But it's possible that was just my imagination. At this age, with the years and memories piling up like cars tangled and mangled in an ice-coated Interstate accident, I have trouble sorting reality from stories, experienced events from imagination. The good news is this....it really doesn't matter. They're all just electrical impulses, unless there was some sort of contract signed at the time.

The occasion for the reintroduction was Mag's 90th birthday celebration in August of 2002. Fred and Denise had been married months before (precise accounting to follow as this scene unfolds). I had been in phone contact with Fred several times, trying to facilitate his trip planning. The details are a little fuzzy, but I remember three distinct calls to Fred regarding his hotel reservations. I made them but when calling to confirm I learned from the desk clerk that Fred had cancelled them. That happened one additional time, same song, different verse, until the third time was the charm....Fred stopped cancelling the reservation.

*Same old goofy Fred...*I judged. I'd heard stories from Michael and Mark about Fred in the meantime, each one reinforcing my image of the hapless uncle. They'd tell of Fred's adventures with the opposite sex. Fred apparently seemed just fine with his widower status, no inclination toward any future permanent relationships. He was still married to Ruth and just waiting to catch up with her in heaven. But there were widows out there who had different intentions. I heard about two: one, a ninety-year-old who coveted Fred's attentions; a second younger woman, in her early seventies, who was trying to corral Fred into a permanent relationship. From 1700 miles away, I couldn't imagine what they could be thinking....trying to capture my goofy uncle?

But Fred could. He reported in excruciating detail their efforts. The older predator offered financial security, something that she gave great weight to and that Fred ignored completely. The younger woman, it turned out to be Denise, was reported to be spinning her web for Fred.

"They're trying to trap me," he reported to Michael.

"How so?" Michael invited further detail.

"When we go up to visit her daughter, she puts us in the same bedroom."

Michael was beginning to get the picture. Fred continued.

"I just don't understand all that wiggling and thrashing down there," Fred explained, his hands wiggling and thrashing 'down there,' Fred's reference to his groinal regions. "But I just pretended to be asleep, or to have a headache," he described his escape route.

Too much information, Michael was thinking. "Good plan," he applauded Fred.

I've used that phrase, 'wiggling and thrashing' a hundred times since, and each time I can see Fred's expressive Italian hands highlighting where 'down there' was. Thank you for that image, Uncle.

Before I forget it, I'd better get this other reference to 'down there' in this report. One day after he'd moved to be near us, Jan was talking to Fred about his career choice of Latin and the Classics. Fred surprised her with this.

"I was actually thinking about a career in science in high school, but one day in chemistry lab I spilled some sulfuric acid 'down there.' That was too close a call so I decided on a future that didn't have sulfuric acid in it."

"Down there?" Jan asked for clarification, she not having heard Fred's characterization.

His eyes dropped to his lap. Jan nodded understanding. We added that phrase into our permanent family lexicon.

Meanwhile back at Mag's 90th. Jan and I drove to the Savannah airport to pick up Fred and Denise, an aunt we had yet to meet. We waited at the end of the long and narrow terminal, searching the crowd that was exiting from the scheduled plane. After the flood of passengers had made their way past us, we began to worry. It was not inconceivable that Fred had found a way to bollix up the trip. But then, from at least one hundred yards away that familiar voice rang out.

"What do they think I am? Some sort of terrorist?" All this accompanied by a furious waving of arms.

The source of this outburst was an old man, bow-legged enough for a Volkswagen to drive through, attired as follows, starting at the top: Wide-brimmed white straw hat, goggle-like tinted sunglasses,

Hawaiian shirt, baggy khaki Bermuda shorts, black socks and garish orange tennis shoes. This level of detail was observable from a distance of one hundred yards.

"That's Fred," I assured Jan who had not at that point had the pleasure.

As he navigated the empty concourse, he wove from side to side, his wheeled suitcase running a slalom course behind him. He'd broken half the handle and the single point of connection afforded little opportunity for balance or control. Hence, the weaving. At his side was his slightly embarrassed bride who was cautioning discretion, his words liable to draw the scrutiny of security officials. Her words had no noticeable effect on Fred who continued his rant until he caught sight of me, arms extended in greeting.

After hugs and introductions, we proceeded to the baggage claim area which was now empty. Folks had gathered their belongings and exited. We walked to the assigned area, but there were only three suitcases on the revolving conveyor, none of them belonging to Fred and Denise. Sensing Fred's anxiety, we opted for Denise as our spokesperson of choice and escorted her to the lost baggage office. While Denise pulled out her claims stubs and completed the proper forms, Fred hovered over the revolving belt. When I say hovered, I mean hovered. His knees were pressed against the side of the baggage claim conveyor, and Fred, nattily attired in his finest travel outfit, was bent over at 90 degrees, his nose inches about the belt, scanning the bags flowing past. Each time the three remaining bags would reappear through the opening, Fred would shout, "Here they come now!!" That scene was repeated at least a dozen times, each reappearance greeted by Fred's optimistic announcement, followed by the disappointing "It's not them."

We figured it was cheap entertainment and distraction while we took care of the required paperwork. Assured that the bags would be located and delivered to the hotel, we retrieved Fred and headed for the hotel. After a side trip to the only open fast food place we could find, we drove into town.

If you were expecting any kind of routine pass through the check-in process, your Fred education continues. I accompanied Fred to the desk, certain after three cycles of making the reservation, that the excitement was over. Not so.

"I'm sorry, we have no reservations for a Mr. Fred Stefano. We have a Mr. Michael Stefano, but he's already checked in," the clerk informed us.

"That's not possible," I protested. "I made those reservations. Here's the confirmation number."

"I'm sorry Mr. Stefano," she misidentified me, "but the Visa credit card you charged the room to was cancelled several weeks ago."

I turned to the culprit. "Fred, is that possible? Did you cancel the credit card?" I needed to know.

"Damn right," he barked. "Those bastards were charging usurious interest rates." Good vocabulary, as always; bad result.

I turned to the clerk. "Do you have any rooms available?"

"Yes sir. We have rooms available."

"Fred, do you have a valid credit card?" I asked.

"No," he mewed in his best George Costanza imitation, the significance of his cancellation beginning to dawn on him.

Denise was a few feet behind us, getting to know Jan and unaware of the problem. I summoned her.

"Denise, do you have a valid credit card?" She did.

"Jan, would you please escort Fred to that couch over there while Denise and I get them a room?"

She did. We did. And the happy couple retired to their marital suite.

"I see what you mean," Jan said as the elevator doors closed behind them. "And you say he's a Mensa?"

"Board certified," I assured her.

You're now thinking that things can't get crazier, right? Stay tuned.

The next morning wacky turned to sad. My cousin and Fred's nephew Michael Stefano reported to us the following scene. A number of the relatives were enjoying the hospitality breakfast in the lobby when an ebullient Fred wandered into the mix. He overloaded a plate with a sample of everything the buffet had to offer,

"Try everything on the first pass," he advised. "See what the really good stuff is."

"Where's Denise?" Michael wondered as Fred wedged his way up to the table.

"She's up in the room," he offered. Then, after downing a forkful of cheeses-covered scrambled eggs, "Crying," he added as an afterthought, or possibly a delayed admission.

"Why?" The entire table was grateful for Michael's unhesitating query.

Fred, always long on candor if short on discretion, offered the explanation. "She wanted pillow talk," he evaded the more accurate characterization of Denise's expectations. "I was too tired so I said 'no.' She got upset and pulled the pillow and blanket off the bed and went to sleep in the bathtub."

Not the answer anyone was expecting.

Michael, in Stefano-direct fashion, "And you let her?"

Fred was taken aback by the question. It had never occurred to him that he should do anything about it. If she wanted to sleep in the tub, he accorded her the freedom to make her own choices. It wasn't unkind of him. It wasn't uncaring. It was just letting Denise make her own choices.

Michael suggested that possibly there might be another way to look at it.

"You need to get back up there, Uncle. You can't leave her alone like that."

Fred was rescued from having to deal with that perspective when Denise exited the nearby elevator door and headed into the dining area. She was distraught, her face red, her eyes puffy and teary, her hands covering her face. The female contingent at the table swung into action, seating her, comforting her, fetching her a cup of tea and generally showing support. Fred took it all in as he finished off his test plate and headed back for the first of several trips to get 'the good stuff.'

"75 days," Denise was sobbing to her huddled comforters. "75 days," she repeated several times before she finally made her point clear. "75 days and this marriage is over."

I'd have to say that Denise was a very exact person. She could have probably gotten it down to hours and minutes if she'd been asked. It was probably born of a Depression-era youth and hardened by years of subsistence living. She carefully guarded her hard-won security. She had developed the practice of keeping a detailed, to the 4th

102

decimal point, accounting of every facet of their lives.....milligrams of dosage of each medicine either of them took; pay and co-pay for each prescription; dollars and cents of the expenses on the trips they took, and the side trips on the trips; her portion of the grocery bill, and his. They kept their finances separate. She paid half the heat bill; Fred paid half. She knew how many cans of soup on the shelf were hers and how many were Fred's. We didn't realize the habit then, only later. For now we knew that Denise was counting the days of her disappointment.

Fred, focused on a stack of maple-syrup drenched pancakes piled high with bacon, missed that turning point in his fortunes.

Michael and his partner Doug, at the instigation of their traveling companion Susan, decided that an intervention was in order. Susan accompanied Denise back to her room to prepare for a trip into town. "Let's go explore the Riverwalk," she proposed. It was a kindness of the first order.

It took a while for Denise to become travel worthy, but eventually the fivesome headed into town. The rest of the family was brought up to speed on the morning's revelations as stories were shared and marveled at. No one was laughing at this episode.

The trip seemed to be a success. Denise calmed down and was in better spirits when the troupe returned. Fred, who'd missed most of the implications of his failure to perform, waded into the family circle, chatting and catching up with relatives he hadn't seen for years. The Fred Show, at least for that occasion, had dropped the curtain on memorable scenes. Michael did pull me aside both to express concern and to entertain with one last story.

The concern first....what should we do about Fred and Denise? My sense on that one was that Fred was just being Fred and that at age 85 he wasn't likely to change much. A line from a Waylon Jennings song came to mind: "It's not his heart, Lord, it's his mind. He didn't mean to be unkind."

The story......As they were concluding their tour of the Riverwalk, they passed an ice cream shop. Fred is incapable of actually passing an ice cream shop. It's in his DNA. He must partake. It being a hot and muggy August afternoon, no one objected. Denise, ever the frugal one, suggested that it would be cheaper for her and Fred to split one of the shop's double side-by-side cones than to purchase two singles. Fred acquiesced, they negotiated which two flavors to order, and completed the transaction...almost. As they exited the store the clerk hollered out, "Hey, wait a minute. You haven't paid for that cone."

To which Fred, disengaging his tongue from his strawberry side, replied "I paid for my half."

A summary of my impressions of Fred from this week's experience: I hadn't been around Fred for 55 years, but nothing he did changed my sense of him as my crazy, lovable uncle.....warm, exuberant, entertaining...but eccentric, very eccentric.

Jan

After she and I shared a few drinks and conversations at Mag's 90th birthday celebration, Denise and I developed a new and unexpected relationship. We'd rarely talked before that, and I'd seen her in person only that one time. Still, we made a connection. She would call frequently, describing the goings-on in their lives. The level of detail was, how shall I put this, in two point type, two thousand words to the page if it were in written form, which it often was, edge to edge on a budget postcard. The lady kept track of things....the itineraries of their trips; the prices, plus tax of their rooms, or bus fares; the diagnoses of all of her, Fred's and many close friends' ailments; and the resulting prescriptions and medications, complete with dosages and unit costs. It was obvious to me that she needed someone to talk to, and I think my role as a physician gave her a sense of confidence in my counsel.

I listened to the detail but what really interested me was the insight she shared about her pre-Fred life. It helped me understand why she was attracted to him. She'd been married long before, ending her tumultuous marriage despite the condemnations of her Catholic faith. It had been that unhappy. She's raised her five children with little help from her ex-husband; was enjoying the growing family of energetic grandchildren; and now found herself wanting her own loving relationship. She'd been guilty long enough.

She met Fred through the daughter of a friend who knew of Fred by way of the senior center connection. They'd gone on a blind date the first time they met. Fred, oblivious to the web she was spinning, waxed eloquent on the topic of his collection of opera music; soared through his travel experiences in the classical venues; revisited sumptuous meals he'd experienced; described almost every pleasure he'd ever known, save any mention of activities regarding 'down

105

there.' Denise must have taken the omission as a gentlemanly exercise in discretion, rather than a portent of disappointments that were to follow.

Denise was clear on what she wanted from Fred. She wanted someone to pay half the costs of living. She kept accurate records of every penny spent, and Fred carried his weight on that subject. She had her side of the cupboard; he had his. She had her cans of soup and vegetables; he had his. She paid her half of the phone bill, including the long-distance calls she initiated; he paid his. She even paid for her half of the bargain two-scoop ice cream cone, and again Fred paid his. Just as Fred had described to the priest who married them, it was a 50-50 deal.

She wanted someone to travel with, and again Fred came through. They traveled the world, albeit sometimes to Denise' great consternation. She'd describe how at almost every stop on the tour bus route, Fred would wander off in search of an ice cream cone (the ice cream cone being Fred's totem). Given his complete lack of spatial intelligence, he could never find his way back to the bus, and the entire tour would be waiting impatiently. "There he is," the shout would eventually ring out, and Fred would wobble toward the waiting fellow travelers. Denise owned him, and therefore the shame she felt at his cluelessness. If it had just been the wandering, it would have been easier to excuse. But Fred also had the habit of correcting the tour bus driver. He'd be explaining in his most professorial air the wonders that lay before the eyes of the riveted crowd, when Fred would interrupt with his unrivetting tool.

"That's incorrect!" Fred would proclaim in a voice that drowned out the professional, "You're telling it wrong." Fred would then explain it the right way, at least Fred's 'right' way. Finally the guide had had all of Fred's corrections that he was willing to tolerate, so as he concluded his monologue at the Coliseum, he opened the floor to questions, part way. "Does anyone have any questions? Except Fred."

One of Fred's mates, who wasn't as challenged as the guide nor as embarrassed as Denise, spoke up. "I don't but Fred can have my question."

So Fred was counted a mixed asset on their travels, but at least he shared the cost of the trip, down to the last penny.

And Denise wanted companionship. She wanted Fred next to her in bed. She wanted some semblance of a sexual relationship. She'd frequently describe the 'little blue pill' (she never used the blatant word Viagra) she'd slip him, and announced proudly that it worked like a charm. But as soon as he deemed his duty done, Fred would hustle out of bed and downstairs to watch TV or listen to his music. No cuddling or lingering for him. He was off to better things. Fred had his own bedroom, and when it was time for sleep, he'd say his prayers and climb in by himself. Denise was as lonely married as she'd been single. She'd been forewarned of his interests (or lack of them), but her hopes had trumped her experience.

The scales still tipped in Fred's balance as long as travel and expense-sharing outweighed his lack of sexual delivery, the score being 2-1. But the scales tipped violently against Fred when he began to come up short on his two long suits.

When I heard of the plans for their latest trip, a safari to Africa, I joked that she must have taken out a healthy life insurance policy and intended to do him in. She sent me copies of the itinerary, and it would have challenged a vibrant and totally continent fifty-year-old. It was obvious that Fred couldn't endure such an ordeal, and I called Denise to express my concern.

"Denise, there's no way that Fred can make that trip," I was direct with her.

She was equally direct with me. "We already paid for it. We can't get a refund. We're going."

I'm imagining the upcoming adventure. Fred on an ordeal of a flight from California to Africa. Fred bouncing over the rutted jungle trails in an open-air Jeep. Fred bouncing out of the Jeep to the delight of the attending lions. Fred sleeping under a mosquito net, then wandering out into the jungle in search of pee privacy, again to the delight of the attending lions. I know Fred likes culture, comfort, good food, music, scintillating conversation. This trip promised the 4 D's of discomfort, dust, dirt and danger; with heat, exhaustion, poor sleeping, primitive toilet and bathing facilities thrown in for good measure.

I couldn't keep quiet. I called Fred.

"Fred, I'm concerned about this upcoming trip to Africa. I don't think it will be good for you. I think it will be hard on you, wear you down. I don't think you should make that trip. Can you just give your ticket to someone else and let them accompany Denise?"

Here's where Fred's boundless optimism got him in trouble. He had always wanted to go on a safari. He'd bought and paid for the ticket. He'd just seen *The Lion King*. The music was splendid. How bad could it be? He could handle it.

"Fred, if the money is the issue, I will be glad to reimburse you for the ticket," I tried.

No deal. Fred was imagining the sight of Kilimanjaro; the breadth of the savannahs; the excitement of the wildlife, the imagined symphonic sound track as background. He was going on a safari.

In the aftermath, once the inevitable had become the reality, Denise needed three hours on the phone to describe the Trip from Hell. I'll not go into all the detail. Just imagine it and it happened. Tale told well enough by this one event. At one point the tour group mutinied, took a vote, and by a unanimous vote (minus Fred and Denise, who weren't invited into the voting booth) demanded that the tour operator throw Fred off the bus. More accurately, drop him off at the next crossroads and send him packing back to the USA. It was that bad. The tour operator, faced with imagined lawsuits no matter which way he decided, opted instead for negotiation, the result being that Denise agreed to take a firmer hand in managing Fred's eccentricities. It wasn't successful in changing Fred's behavior, but at least hinted at good intentions on the operator's part. The mutiny was salved if not eliminated.

Now I'm beginning to understand Denise' scoring system, Fred's down 0-3, and another piece of bad news might hit the tipping point. The next one didn't. The one after that did.

A couple of weeks later Denise called in a tizzy. Fred had met this 'really nice guy' at the senior center bridge table. He was going on a mission to Haiti and needed financial support to help build a school there. Would Fred help him carry on this work of mercy, to the tune of $3500? Fred had written out the check before Denise got wise to the caper and called me.

"He won't give me the checkbook," she concluded after giving me the details of the scam.

"Let me talk to him," I suggested.

"Fred, this is Jan. Denise was telling me about your desire to support a mission to Haiti."

That launched Fred into a parroting of the sales pitch he'd been given. "It's our responsibility to our unfortunate brothers,"

Fred was dead on target.

"I have to support him."

Hard to argue with the spirit behind that. Rather than point out the likelihood that Fred was being conned, I offered an alternative.

"Fred, I've seen your finances, and you can't afford to donate that kind of money, even though it is very generous of you to consider it. You need your money to last through your retirement, *and to meet your half of the marital living expenses,* I felt like adding. Fred hadn't needed a share of Denise's living expenses. He'd been provided a life tenancy in a beautiful home that Ruth's son Gary had built for them. Denise was the one who'd sold Fred on sharing the expenses of her home. But that horse was out of the barn and not the topic of today's concern.

"Fred, Steve and I can afford to help that mission. You tell that nice man to call me and we'll discuss his needs. Okay? Fred? You there? Fred?"

In retrospect I think Fred was considering the donation a downpayment on his sainthood application; that he wasn't planning on a long life on this earth and was anxious to join Ruth and his beloved dog Peetie in heaven; and that he was reluctant to pass up this opportunity for greatness.

"Are you still there, Fred?" I needed to clarify.

"Yes," came the meek reply.

"I want you to give Denise the checkbook now, okay? Will you hand it to her?"

After a brief hesitation, "If I have to."

"Thank you Fred." One tipping point avoided, one to go.

The next few calls had an unsettling nature. Denise would always initiate the call and now the topic of conversation focused on Fred's frailties, and on Denise's fading ability to cope with them.

Fred was a messy eater.

Fred wasn't, well, clean. This was an illusion to an incontinence issue that was worsening with time.

Fred spends too much time at the senior center.

Fred doesn't spend enough time at the senior center.

The calls were always interspersed with shouting and 'Give me the phone' and the unmistakable message that it was a very unhappy household. The spoken and unspoken theme was that Denise was rerunning the calculations with new numbers for variables. Fred as an asset was sliding into Fred as a liability.

The tipping point came a few weeks later. Again the call was from Denise, and this time she was in tears. Here is that story:

Fred had been showering before his daily visit to the senior center. Denise had told him repeatedly how she wanted the shower cleaned after he was finished. She wanted the walls squeegeed after each shower. Fred was getting a *D* when she wanted an *A* performance. She'd had all she could take and on the day in question had gone into the shower to show Fred 'one more time' how she wanted it done. The two of them struggled over the squeegee and in the process Fred took an incidental whack to the forehead with the contested appliance. Medicated as he was, Fred bled profusely. Both of them were mad as he exited the shower, dressed and hustled off to a more receptive place. When Fred arrived at the center, his face was covered with dried blood.

"Fred, what happened?" the concerned staffer asked him.

"Denise hit me with the squeegee," was Fred's innocent if damning reply.

State law took over. It required, under penalty of severe punishment, that caregivers report any suspected incident of senior abuse. A few minutes later Denise answered her doorbell to find two uniformed officers facing her.

"Denise Thompson?" they began. Her first reaction was *Something's happened to Fred.* The reality was that something was happening to her.

"You have the right to remain silent. Anything you do say can and may be used against you in a court of law."

The tipping point had been reached, and Fred was now sliding out the back of the dump truck to an uncertain fate. Denise had decided that he needed to be in a care facility...she hadn't signed up to become his caregiver. She had worked hard all her life, the later years as a caregiver, and she wasn't going to spend her 'golden' years doing it for free. She further calculated that her assets would be at risk in providing for Fred's care, and that was a sacrifice she was unwilling to make. Her romantic aspirations were now shoved into the backseat as her financial considerations moved up to shotgun.

She planned to divorce Fred, which meant she planned to evict him to his own devices. Her imagination began creating the comfort zone that her conscience would need.

"I think Fred might have murdered Ruth," she rearranged the facts she'd heard about Ruth's passing. *A lady couldn't be expected to live with that kind of threat* gave her the room she needed to act.

When the conversation finally ended, I tracked down Steve who was in his office writing.

"Stevie, we need to get Fred out of that house and back here where we can look after him. He's in trouble."

Steve

As Jan spelled out the latest chapter of the Fred and Denise Show, I allowed myself the luxury of a few hours of anger at Denise. She was the one who had manipulated Fred out of his beautiful, free-for-life home. She was the one who wanted to get married. She was the one who had needed a cuddler and a Viagra-infused lover and a financial supporter. Fred had just wanted to be Fred. And now that she'd managed to maneuver Fred out of his life and into hers, she was ready for the next maneuver....to throw Fred, not off but under the bus.

The anger wasn't helping much, and this situation needed fixing, not judging. As I cooled off a little, I could understand Denise's motivation. She'd struggled all her life and now Fred was threatening her secure future. "Done's done," as my ole pappy used to say. Since the wedding was an established fact (I'd seen the wedding pictures and heard the stories to prove it), and since I didn't have a time machine so that we could go back to point where this whole sad story could be written differently, my ole pappy's advice seemed to be pointing to, "Fix what is, not what you think it oughta be."

I called Denise. She was fearful. Was this the avenging angel calling to rain down fire and brimstone? A few minutes of conversation revealed that her fear was that Fred would seek some financial support from her. I assured her that we recognized her concerns and that we had no expectation that she would support Fred.

"Denise, I'm calling so that I can figure out how to help you and Fred. We don't want either you or Fred to have to be afraid. It's clear to us that your marriage did not work out the way either of you hoped it would, and we'd like to help in the transition to what's next for both of you. Jan and I are committed to moving Fred to a care facility and I just need to know what kind of resources he has that can be used for that purpose. Can you send me copies of Fred's financial records?"

While Denise's primary motivation was self-preservation, she seemed relieved that there might be a solution that protected Fred as well. She became our ally in the effort.

My next call was to Mary, Fred's step-daughter and biggest fan. Mary and her siblings, children and grandchildren had been Fred's family for the past 50 years, much closer to him than we had been. I knew of Mary but don't think I'd ever met her in person. I made the call.

<u>Mary</u>

Lisa and I had been worried about the way Fred's marriage to Denise had been going lately. In the early months, I became the frequent recipient of her animated descriptions of the state of affairs in their household. I'd get a call from Denise reporting excitedly that she and Fred, now sanctioned under the banner of Matrimony, had just had sex. The phone would ring shortly after that announcement and it would be Fred, reporting the same event. No filters on either of those two innocents. They came at it from different perspectives....Denise to report small victories, a plan come together; Fred to share another small joy in his life. As the Gary Larson cartoon had it: *Same planet, Different worlds.* Oh, there were the complaints from Denise that Fred, once having performed his version of 'it,' would hop out of bed and hustle downstairs to read, watch TV or listen to his 'precious music.' But some was better than none, so things seemed passable.

But passable was turning into muddy lately. Their travel was now limited by Fred's declining health. The African safari was by all accounts an unmitigated disaster and pretty much the end of their travel years. That was a huge disappointment to Denise. Fred's health issues were also adding to burdens that Denise had not anticipated. She was turning into a caregiver instead of a partner.

One day I got a call from Fred's nephew Stephen. I of course knew of him through Fred and his brothers and sister, and I think he was with Fred one time in Cincinnati, but that would have been when he was a pre-teenager. The call was out of the blue. After a few minutes of introductions, he got to the purpose of his call. Denise had gotten to the end of her rope with Fred, and was now concerned that Fred's frailties and his need for increased care were more than she could handle. I don't know whether or not she had told him this, but he

115

seemed certain that she was concerned that her assets would be required if she did in fact put Fred in an assisted living center, and that she was unwilling to risk her future in that way. So she had decided to get a divorce. Fred would be out on his own. He asked me if I could check in on Fred and assess the situation. Lisa and I went to see Fred later that day. We took him to dinner and asked how things were going. Fred, who had always had a sunny outlook on even the dimmest of prospects, seemed discouraged. The divorce hadn't been mentioned to him yet.

I called Steve back and told him that we agreed that we needed to get Fred out of that unhappy situation. Lisa and I checked out options in our area, but found none that were within Fred's financial capabilities. I told Steve that we would be willing to subsidize Fred's living expenses, but he thought that unnecessary. Steve's mother lived in a wonderful retirement center very near him, and it was both affordable and convenient. We made the decision for Fred, who by this stage was beyond deciding things for himself. Stephen prepared the apartment, and Lisa, Jake and I organized things on the Fred end. Denise, relieved that her burden was about to be lifted, and that Fred was placing no demands for spousal support, packed Fred's bags and had him polished up and standing by the door when we arrived to pick him up for the trip to his new home.

Denise's parting words were," Have a nice trip, Fred. You're going to visit your sister for a couple of weeks."

We didn't think adding to her description would improve the travel any, so we waved goodbye and headed for the airport.

Fred

The day Ruth died, the heart went out of me.

There are no other words to explain it. I might just as well have died that day myself, but my body wasn't ready.

Ruth had been the center of my life for over forty years. She was where I could trust to place my love. And she never abandoned me. In each other we both found peace. Her last two years were so hard on her. It was painful to watch the diseases wear her away. At times she appeared to lose faith in me, to become distrustful. But I knew it was the dementia, not Ruth, that was in control at that stage. When she was finally released from these earthly bonds, her spirit soared into the heavens. Her ashes we entrusted to the Pacific, according to her wishes. I made it known that when my time came, I wanted my spirit to join her in heaven, my work, and my ashes to follow her into that great ocean. I trusted that task to my family.

For a while, I tried to act as if life went on. I attended soccer games and family dinners. I played bridge at the senior center. I was Fr. Siro's favorite lector and was a regular again at church. But something vital had changed. Try as I would to find it, the joy had gone out of things. That is not to say that there was no enjoyment left. Pavarotti's tenor voice could still lift my spirits to near the heavens. A good ice cream cone, and they were all good, could take me back to my childhood days. But it wasn't the same as before.

My family tried their mightiest to buoy my spirits. At one point they even tried to fix me up with another woman. I wish that hadn't happened. I was bonded for life and beyond with Ruth. I had no need or desire for another relationship.

But something more than my heart went out of me. My physical strength began to ebb. I couldn't walk like I used to. I couldn't carry the things I used to. I couldn't hear the closest conversation. I couldn't see as well, although my nephew Stephen would sometimes help with that. He'd say, "Uncle. I'm going to work a miracle. I'm going to restore your sight. " Then he'd take off my glasses, clean them clear as a crystal, and put them back on me. That was a small miracle that I was grateful for.

I couldn't sleep soundly like I used to. Hells bells, I couldn't even control my bladder or my bowels. That was so embarrassing. I know part of that was aging, but not all of it.

And it wasn't just my body. My mind took the same downhill turn. I couldn't remember things. I couldn't find the words to match my thoughts. Can you imagine what it was like for me to have a clear thought inside my head, but not find the words to speak it? I was becoming useless.

Maybe it was by conscious choice, or maybe it was all I had left, but I gradually just let it all go. I couldn't control any of it. So I just lived with what was left. I agreed to marry Denise, the woman the kids wanted me to meet. I didn't want to do it, but I gave in. We had some good enough times together. We traveled all over the world. We even went on a safari to Africa. It hot and dusty and a jarring ride in that contraption we rode in, but it was worth the effort. We saw every imaginable animal that Africa had to offer. That was our last big trip though. It was becoming too hard to make that kind of effort.

Our marriage took a turn for the worse after that trip. Or maybe it would be more accurate to say that Denise finally realized that she wanted more than I had to give. I felt badly for her. She'd been alone a long time and wanted to be close to someone again. I didn't have it in me.

I remember a lot of yelling. "Do this. Don't do that." I just wanted her to leave me alone. Finally Mary and Lisa and Jake rescued both of us from that unhappy state. They picked me up and took me to live the Margaret and Jan and Stephen. I think it was supposed to be just a visit, but when I got there they had a room all made up for me, *Casa Di Stefano* it said on the door. The walls were hung with pictures of all my family: Mama, Fluffy, Albert, Carl and Vic, Joe and Margaret. I remember being surprised when Stephen told me that this was my new home. Mostly I was relieved. I didn't want to go back to California and Denise. I just wanted a quiet place where I could spend my days in prayer, preparing my hoped-for entry to the next world.

Steve

Title this chapter 'The Beginning of the Adventure.' The weary passengers climbed down the rickety stairs of the 19 passenger regional aircraft, which Fred later referred to as 'the tube of death,' an unsettling reference to the plane's narrow dimensions and thundering noise level. Fred plopped into a waiting wheelchair and the foursome, Mary, Lisa, Jake and Fred, made their way into the terminal. Hugs were exchanged, introductions made, and we headed for the retirement home and the new *Casa di Stefano*.

"Where are we going?" was Fred's question, but 'When do we eat?' was what he meant.

"We've got a great new room for you where Margaret lives, and we're going there now. They'll have a lunch ready for us."

That's what he needed to know. Mary and Lisa unloaded Fred while I retrieved my mother from her apartment. The reunion in the lobby was joyous. We lugged Fred's two suitcases onto a trolley and headed for his apartment. The 'Casa di Stefano" sign on the door delighted him. We walked in, he surveyed the surroundings and declared them splendid. Now came what could have been the tricky part.

"This is your new home, Fred," I introduced the concept.

He looked at me with the obvious question on his face.

I got straight to the point. "Denise can no longer provide the care you need and deserve. We're going to take care of you now. You never have to worry about anything ever again. You're with your family and we'll make sure you have everything you need."

I'd have to say that the next moment was one of the most amazing I've ever experienced. Fred just drew in a deep breath, looked around once again, scanned the wall and took in the photographs of Mama, his brothers and sisters, and said, "Okay." He took the news of this major change in his life and absorbed it in a matter of seconds. I think Fred was wearing down and didn't need to control anything anymore. If you want my read, I'd say that Fred's lifelong quest had been to fit into family. He'd found it at times with his mother, at the orphanage for a brief while, with his sister and her family, with Ruth and her family, and now he'd found it again. Everyone in the room experienced it as we watched Fred go into what appeared to be perfect peacefulness. Unless you've been on a desert island and seen a man washed ashore and gratefully hugging the warm sand beneath him, you don't get many moments like that in a lifetime.

"So when do we eat," was his next obvious question, and the signal that all was right in Fred's world.

He settled into the new surroundings and routine with ease. First up was the feeding schedule...breakfast on the table at 8 AM, lunch at noon, and dinner at 4:30 PM. Fred locked those numbers into his wiring, and I don't think he ever missed a meal. Across the hallway from the dining room was the ice cream parlor, a bonus of unimaginable importance to Fred.

"You mean I can help myself any time I want to?" he sought reassurance when I introduced him to the Boundless Dispenser of Frozen Gold, the unattended soft ice cream machine.

"Any time. As much as you want," I assured him. He took me literally, and he never had a meal, breakfast, lunch or dinner, where he didn't have an overfilled cone afterwards, and many times before. It wasn't always pretty. The cones had a way of dripping onto his pants, requiring the addition to his wardrobe of enough changes to get him through until laundry day. I later learned to buy Fred's pants with an elastic waistband, since this unguarded fountain of delight led to an immediate and substantial weight gain.

I had hoped that the local Catholic Church would welcome Fred with open arms, providing this saint-in-waiting with a ride to Sunday mass. I visited St. James Catholic Church, the only one in town with a permanent staff and office.

"I'm sorry. We can't help you," the pastor said. "The retirement center is in Prince of Peace parish. You'll need to talk to Fr. Mike."

Fr. Mike never did return one of my four phone messages. They were very prompt in getting Fred a year's worth of collection envelopes, but not once did they get him to one of their services. On rare occasion a retired priest would deliver communion, and Fred appreciated that, but he had to settle for a daily mass that was broadcast on a religious TV channel. To put it kind terms, the Church didn't return the love.

Fred settled into a very comfortable daily schedule:

Wake-up, dress and breakfast by 8. Ice cream cone after, and sometimes before.

Back to his room where the TV was set to play one of his music videos, Pavarotti being his favorite with a Belgian violinist, a Lawrence Welk type whose name escapes me at the moment and whose music was German-Ooompah to the max, close behind in second place. Fred was unable to understand the controls, but between the staff and me, we were able to run that VCR player almost constantly. Fred was absorbed in the music, already two steps toward his heavenly goal. Several of his neighbors, including Little Ralph, as distinguished from Big Ralph, would join him on occasion to share in his joy of the music. There was the occasional complaint from the next-door neighbor that the volume was too loud, but Fred would sit by quietly while the staff lowered the sound level from "Booming" to "Elevator."

Noon...down the hall for lunch, again with the ice cream, on top of whatever dessert he'd downed with lunch.

Back to his room for several hours of prayer and reading of his daily missal.

During the afternoons Fred would usually fall asleep in his chair, sometimes making it to his bed for a horizontal rest. He'd invariably wrap himself around one of his favorite Teddy bears, and the staff who came to wake him for dinner would have to separate the two before sending him toward the dining room. At one point a young man on the care staff decided to try to train Fred to answer the phone, by this time a technological challenge, to get his call to dinner. It ultimately proved unsuccessful for two reasons. First, Fred wasn't very good at answering the phone, and secondly, he often needed 'freshened up' before he was presentable for a social environ

The nightly exodus to dinner was a sight to behold. The doors of the dining room were scheduled to open at 4:30. Folks with little to do after their naps would begin the move around 4, and the mass migration would commence about 4:20. It was wall-to-wall chaos with a mixture of slow walkers, walkers with walkers or canes, motorized scooters and wheelchairs, some going forward, some actually going backwards because it was easier to scoot along that way. No one's life nor limb was safe in that anarchy. Anyone foolish enough to try to pass a slower mover would invariably cause some version of a crash, either walkers into one another, or into the furniture that lined the hallways. If a guy were visiting during that period, an alternate route was the only sane course.

There was the occasional mystery to be solved. Fred announced one day that Father Siro had assured him that he had put Fred into his will, to the tune of $650,000, and that Fred was charged to do good work with the bounty. There may conceivably be some seemingly sanctimonious larcenous lawyer feasting on the priest's legacy, but we decided to chalk that one up to delusion.

Fr. Siro also seemed to be the source of Fred's most consistent belief. Fred was absolutely convinced that he was a saint. It went so far that at one point Fred took to 'the laying on hands of hands', passing the blessing of an anointed one on to the other residents of The Home. That didn't sit too well with several of the other residents who considered themselves Fred's equal or superior in the sanctified department. Word got back to us through the staff, and Jan had a sit-down with Fred.

"Fred, you are making some of the other residents uncomfortable when you put your hands on them to bless them," seemed like an approach that would appeal to Fred's considerate nature.

"But I have to. I'm a saint," presented Jan's next challenge. She was up to it.

"Fred, you can't be a complete saint yet. You have to be dead to actually become a saint," she delivered in her confident and calm physician manner.

"That's the miracle of it all," Fred countered. "I'm a saint and I'm not even dead."

This one runs deep, Jan understood. She went deep with her response.

"Fred, you won't be able to stay here if you keep blessing people in the dining room and hallway. You won't be able to eat here with Little Ralph and Eldon and Jacquie." And then the clincher, "And you won't have access to the ice cream machine. You can be a saint, and you can pray for your friends, but you have to do it in your room. Okay?"

Deep did it. Fred had never been under the illusion that being a saint was easy work. After all most of them ended up pierced with arrows, tossed to the lions or burned at the stake. If being a closet saint was what it took to fulfill his destiny, and in the meantime maintain access to the ice cream machine, then that was a sacrifice he could live with.

"Okay" set him on the road to continued residency in The Home.

Sundays featured Mag and Fred over to our place for dinner and a rousing run at the Los Angeles Times crossword puzzle. This was a full contact sport, at least for Mag. She was alert, poised on the edge of her seat, straining to hear the clue so that she could be sure to fire out the answer while Fred was still trying to decipher what we'd said. There were so many funny scenes at that table.

Hearing was an issue, so when I'd read a clue, it was fascinating to observe what was heard. Example. I said "ala carte." Fred heard "Trolley car." Mag corrected him with, "No, he said 'volley carp.'"

One day Fred, as was his wont, began singing. This time is wasn't the usual Gregorian chant. It was his personal version of "Home on the Range," which contained this memorable line:

"And the clouds are not cloudy all day."

Another mangling of the language occurred on a Sunday after a Nebraska football game the day before.

Fred mused, "I never thought I'd be a Bushwacker."

"What do you mean, Fred, a Bushwacker?"

"You know," Fred said, "a Nebraska Bushwacker, Big Red. You know."

'That'd be a Cornhusker, Fred, a Nebraska Cornhusker."

"Oh," he was resignedly corrected.

Trying to follow Fred's train of thought was like trying to trail a mouse through a darkened maze . . . . very few clues about where he was headed or might turn next. It was sort of a stream of consciousness, without the continuity of a stream. It was more like a stuttering of consciousness. And sometimes his thoughts were clear and eloquently spoken, but the detectives trying to understand them had to guess at the context.

I'd find short sentences written on sticky notes. To wit:

My Dear Brother in Christ Jesus, I humbly praise St. Siro for our working so diligently in helping me to obtain sainthood. You will always have my love in the name of our Triune God. Or,

Mio Caro Amico: Please look at our wedding pictures!!! I feel you are part of my familia. Much love and blessings. The 'amico" indicates a male addressee; Fred knew his genders in five languages. I'm thinking maybe it was addressed to Little Ralph. I liked the 'familia' net he threw out over whoever it was. Or

I had 4 transient ischemic attacks. I was told if I had a 4th I would die. One day I was not sent in, basically they were, stutter, stutter, *I was not allowed on the landing barge because they feared I'd fall in and get drowned.* His failing brain was locked onto a solid event, and seemed to span a period of 64 years. Someone was home, even as they say, if lights were out.

One day I had the sad chore of informing Mag that her friend Mary Winifred had passed away. I read her the obituary from the local paper. Fred had known Mary Winifred and was paying rapt attention. When I read out the dates of her birth and death, Fred remarked, "That's interesting. She died on the same day that I did," getting the part about the shared birthday right but erring a little on the state of his own health.

Some days the oldsters shared tales of sympathy for other oldsters, as in Mag's offering regarding a Savannah friend, the mother of brother John's second wife:

"Poor Gertrude. She has no life. She opens her garage door, opens a folding chair and just sits there and watches traffic go by."

Fred didn't seem sufficiently moved by that description. Mag thought it sufficiently sad as it was, adding for emphasis, "She lives on a dead end street" to conclude that exchange.

On his 'good' days Fred could still tell a coherent story. We knew that the second love of his life, behind his wife Ruth, was his dog Peetie. One Sunday we learned of Peetie's claim to dog sainthood. Fred explained the source of Peetie's renown. Each night before bed, Fred would fall to his knees in bedtime prayer. Peetie would kneel, Fred's description, next to him and appeal to whatever god dogs beseech. Fred, who that evening had been alarmed by a PBS special on the San Andreas Fault, was praying to be spared from the inevitable quake. Peetie seemed more intent than usual that night, whimpering his prayers in a most fervent manner. That night an earthquake measuring 6.6 on the Richter scale shook the Bay area. San Jose was 'miraculously' untouched. Fred shared with fellow church members the role of Peetie in the community's salvation, and he was henceforth known among that small circle as "Peetie the Praying Dog That Saved San Jose."

Mary told of a different handle for Peetie. She and Lisa were frequent visitors to their home. On their first visit they developed the impression that Denise had chosen a unique splotchy pattern for her carpeting. Closer investigation revealed that Peetie shared Fred's incontinence issue, and the carpet pattern was one of his creation, hence "Peetie the Peeing Puppy."

Fred was involved in one incident that resulted in an eviction. Fortunately Fred was not the evictee.

I got a call one evening. "Steve, can you come over here? Fred's been attacked."

I hadn't seen that one coming. "Is he okay?"

"Oh, he's fine. We just need to fill out some paperwork."

"I'm on my way," I told Gloria.

As I drove into the lot I parked next to a police cruiser that had just arrived. I walked in beside the young officer. Gloria met us at the door.

"This is Fred's nephew," she introduced me.

"I'd like to take the statement of the lady involved first," he said. "I'll come down to your uncle's apartment to get his statement in a few minutes if that's okay with you." With that he followed Gloria to the perp's apartment.

Greg, Fred's best buddy and the maintenance supervisor at The Home, was there to explain the events to me.

"Where's Fred?" I needed to know first.

"He's fine," Greg assured me. "He's down having his second ice cream cone." All was clearly under control.

"So what is this all about?" I asked Greg.

"Darndest thing I've ever seen around here," he began. "Fred was sitting at dinner with his usual friends. Without any warning, Mrs. X (we shall preserve her anonymity) came up behind Fred's chair, grabbed the hair on both sides of his head, and started shaking his head and screaming, "San Jose. San Jose."

Fred, who was expecting dessert and not a beheading, screamed back, "Get her off me. Get her off me."

"One of the staffers quickly came to Fred's aid and pulled the assailant off, the only damage being to his pride and composure. No one was hurt, but the entire dining room had just been exposed to more excitement than we'd seen since, well, ever."

"Do you have any idea what triggered the outburst?"

"I doubt we'll ever get a straight story," Greg correctly judged, "but we'll see what the officer comes up with."

Long story told short, we never did find out what caused the outburst. She couldn't explain it. Fred couldn't explain it. Love unrequited conceivably, since she lived across the hall from Fred. Or vengeance of an opera hater. Or the Wrath of God delivered upon a liberal humanist by a vengeful Person of Faith. Who knows? When it came time for corporate policy to kick in, Mrs. X's son was given thirty days to find her new quarters. Fred didn't find it in his heart to protest her eviction.

"She's crazy," was all he had to say on the matter.

It wasn't long before I realized that I was in the front row of a grand drama. I knew I needed to share the theater with all of those who loved Fred. I began to write a short column titled "This Week in Fred," which I sent to the "Fred List."

Here are the columns that I wrote:

This Week in Fred I
Janet Jackson's Wardrobe Malfunction, Bah! Nuthin!

On Sunday morning one could not have guessed at the week to come. All was as normal as things could be during the opening decade of the century. Christians were aknee (crossword for kneeling); golfers attired in pink and lime dotted the manicured landscape; football fans were atwitter at the prospects of opening week of college ball; and a few outed Republicans were busy spinning Family Values Sexual Scandal, Volume Thirty-Three. What could go wrong?

The first hints came Monday morning when Nurse Carla spotted Fred emerging from his room, head down and food on his mind.

"Fred. Where are you headed in that outfit?"

"Breakfast" was his meek response, as if there were any place else one would go.

"Fred, you've got your pajama tops on over your shirt. Let's take that off and you can be on your way."

"Okay."

No harm. No foul.

Tuesday's episodes might have suggested to the astute observer that "maybe there's something new in the air."

Nurse Jana entered Fred's bedroom to steer him to lunch, not that he needed encouragement to head for the chow hall but only to alert him to the fact that "now's the time." She found Fred on his back in bed, covered from head to waist in a black nylon laundry bag, and flailing to free himself from the makeshift straight jacket.

"Stupid pajamas" he was muttering.

Jana intervened, lifted the offending shroud from Fred's head, dressed him and he proceeded, head down, to shuffle toward the lunch line. He would have said "thank you," but the picture of soup, Jello salad and sandwich bled off the sides of Fred's screen and there was no room for other images or considerations.

Wednesday's caper could have tested the limits of the non-custodial staff that entered his room that morning. The rehabilitation consultant from Alpha Rehab, arriving for the second of her thrice-weekly appointments, discovered Fred, standing buck naked, in the center of the kitchen. Unflappable these rehab types. She calmly dressed Fred then put him through his paces. Fred muttered the whole time, wishing in "Are we there yet?" tones that these cursed exercises would be over so that he could head for lunch.

I arrived Thursday morning to carry out the daily ministrations to find Fred abed, on his back, hugging his Teddy bear. When he became aware of my presence, he started laughing almost uncontrollably.

"Guess what happened to me last night?"

I took that as a rhetorical offer and allowed as how he should just go ahead and tell me. Guessing in these situations rarely breathes the same air as the reality underlying the offer.

"My pants fell off." More uncontrolled laughter.

"Where?" says I.

"In the food line."

"When?"

"At dinner last night."

Now I'm a little worried. Wednesday night is "Special Dinner" night at the home. "Special" is a misleading word. The dinner that night is a buffet line that requires The Home's residents . . . canes, walkers, scooters, oxygen bottles and all . . . to stumble through a maze to acquire their various-colored wriggly salads and somehow schlep their bounty to a table. "Special" might have been coined by The World's Funniest Home Video staff. Point being, all eyes, which don't have much

131

else to do, are on the line, and that's where Fred's most recent wardrobe malfunction occurred.

"Did you have underwear on?" I asked briskly.

"Oh yes," he replied. Who wouldn't have underwear on? he thought.

Given Fred's level of awareness, I figured I'd test that piece of information against a more reliable source. Fortunately, almost everyone in The Home was a witness, and they all reported that he had indeed been attired in his "unnerwear." Maude reported that his very natty tan shorts had dropped to his ankles. Fred started laughing; the observing multitude laughed with him, not at him, a kindlier bunch nowhere to be found on the face of the Earth. One of the staff rushed discreetly to his assistance, tugging his shorts up into their original upright and locked position, and the "Special Dinner" resumed, a little more "Special" than usual.

Given Fred's probation on the "Saint" thing, I inquired as to the management's reaction to the unseemly event. No one took offense, or at least mentioned it, and as far as they were concerned, it was just one more in a string of Fred's colorful contributions to life at The Home. It didn't even go into his record.

Friday's contribution set the capstone on the notion that we are entering new times. Ginny, the charge nurse that morning, went to fetch Fred for breakfast. She entered his room to find him, again in the center of the kitchen, this time attired from head to waist, in a large white plastic garbage bag. Fred's "unnerwear" was not part of the morning's ensemble.

"Fred. What are you doing?"

"Putting on my shirt."

I asked Fred what to expect for the theme of this week's excellent adventures. He said it would be obvious.

Stay tuned.
And it could have been a lot worse. See next page:

132

Man arrested at North Platte school wearing garbage bag

BY DIANE WETZEL

THE NORTH PLATTE TELEGRAPH

NORTH PLATTE, Neb. — A man wearing only a plastic garbage bag was arrested at Adams Middle School early Friday morning.

The man, identified as James L. Tollat, gave a false name and several Social Security numbers when confronted by police.

"He told the officers he wasn't wearing clothes because he didn't have any," said Martin Gutschenritter, chief of police. "The bag only covered him from the waist up."

Tollat was taken to the Lincoln County Jail, where jail staff recognized him from a previous arrest last week and identified him.

"He gave us the name James Lee Schroeder," Gutschenritter said. "He was arrested last week for creating a disturbance in a local store."

Apparently, Tollat offered to sell marijuana to personnel at the store, Gutschenritter said.

"He was wearing underwear on his head at the time," Gutschenritter said.

Tollat was cited for disturbing the peace, processed and released in that incident.

Emergency Support Services located a spot for Tollat at a mission in Lincoln, and arranged his transport there.

Gutschenritter said no charges would be filed for the incident at the school.

This Week in Fred II
... the forbidden fruit

As you may have guessed, the theme of the week is "the forbidden fruit." It's been a good news, bad news week.

The good news . . . Fred's happy. He's safe. He's secure. He has no worries. And he can pray to his heart's content. He's well fed . . . up fourteen pounds since his last weigh-in. It's mainly the ice cream. He has, and exercises, unlimited access to the ice cream machine. It's a pre-breakfast and post-meal routine that is unstoppable. He's a treat-seeking missile. And what's the harm?

We've been to Walmart several times to buy clothes in larger girths, from 36" waists to 38" waists to 40" waists and finally to elastic waists in sweat pants.

Here's the bad news . . . Fred's clearly failing. He experiences shortness of breath very easily. The incontinence continues unabated, which severely limits his social options. And last week he was reported roaming the halls naked . . . well, not exactly naked. He had selected for his ensemble his slippers and his HELP button.

And he had developed the disturbing habit (disturbing to his neighbor) of pounding on the walls at night, not a good habit for continuing lodging privileges at The Home.

"They" (the geriatricians) have a name for this . . . something like grand delusions. He was afflicted before during his "sainthood" phase. We decided to reintroduce the anti-depressant that cured him before. It worked like a charm again this time, and he's sleeping through the night absent his recent new habits. A good thing.

I took him to the doctor today. She observed a significant change from his May visit. She said she could hear heart valve problems, and she ran an EKG. Main problem is, there's not much she can or would do at his age. No caths. No surgery. No stress test. So she's thinking that she'll limit her intervention to meds to make sure he's without discomfort.

That's about it for This Week in Fred. Here's a picture of him and his big sister enjoying the last of summer's warmth on the deck last Sunday:

And here's the last of the bad news . . . Fred owes the Home $3.99 for damage to one of the decorations in the lobby.

Notice the teeth marks indicating the decoration did not goes easily into this dark night.

As Paul Harvey would say, "Now for the rest of the story.

One of the staff noticed Fred sitting on the couch in the entryway, evidencing some agitation. She walked over to find Fred trying to chew the bite that he'd just wrested from the niggardly fruit.

"This damn apple is stale," he complained while continuing to chew, furiously.

"Spit that bite out," she suggested as she observed the cavity in the table decoration. "I'll get you a fresher one."

Giving up a bite of anything was against Fred's religion, but the promise of a fresher version won the day.

"Thank you," he graciously offered as he handed her the mouthful of the forbidden fruit. Grateful and courteous even under stress.... that was Fred.

This Week in Fred III
Christmas in Wonderland

(Important tip . . . have a Kleenex handy for this one)

Here's the Wonderland part.

It's been a few weeks since there's been much novel-worthy to report. Fred's new med cocktail has dimmed his delusions, and he's no longer acting in ways that threaten his tenancy at The Home. He's settled into a routine of food, ice cream and prayer. He's also quite interactive with the commercials on TV. He's in an ongoing conversation with them, accompanied by background music from his CD collection.

Mag's mantra du jour is: "You know, I'm beginning to feel a slight affection for The Brother." She's ready at a moment's notice to exit her secluded den and venture down the hall, trying to remember where Fred's apartment is.

The mirth has come at the expense of two near-deaf oldsters trying to communicate in the presence of a transcriber. As in:

Mag, referring to Grampa Albert's mangled English of "very good", "Belly goot!"

Fred's query, "What belly fruit?", or

The answer to a crossword was "penguin." From the other side of the table, "What got mangled?"

Yesterday's highlight was this exchange:

Mag was reciting a Robert Frost poem, sometimes getting it right from some memory store, sometimes not so much. When she got to the "in the gloamin'" part, she stopped.

"I wonder what a gloamin' means?"

Fred snaps from across the table, "It means they're very rich."

137

Mag gets her frequent puzzled look just right and asks, "How does it mean that?"

Fred replies as if the answer should be obvious, "Anybody'd have to be rich to have their own doorman."

We look at each other, momentarily stopped by that logic, until, "No Fred, that's 'gloamin', not doorman."
You get the picture. It's really funny, you couldn't hire a Hollywood writer to come up with this stuff, and everybody has a "belly goot" laugh.

Here's the Christmas part:

A few weeks ago The Home was visited by the choir and orchestra from Kearney High School. The denizens had gathered in the assembly hall on the third floor and into the arena shuffled Fred, moving imperceptibly behind his walker. Then, to the horror of the multitude, he stumbled and splatted as if part of the warm-up act, and hush descended on the crowd. Someone alertly pushed their call-button pendant and an aide rushed in to assist. Fred was down and moaning, trying to get up but to no avail. He was eventually righted, and although complaining of a sore hand, he wanted to stay for the entertainment. The kids in the orchestra were horrified by the event and much in sympathy with Fred's distress. Their concern was compounded when Fred asked if they could play a Beethoven piece, and they had to confess that they didn't have any Beethoven in their repertoire.

Jan took Fred to the hospital the next day where he was diagnosed and treated for a broken finger. That has healed quickly and he's fine, fingerwise.

Monday night of this past week was The Home's annual Christmas extravaganza: food, treats, lights, and a presentation from the balcony in the entry area by the aforementioned Kearney High School orchestra and choir. The conductor scanned the crowd from above and then asked, "Where's Fred?" He had searched the crowd for that familiar face and found it missing. Pam said she'd go retrieve him. He was on his couch, napping in a seated position.

"C'mon Fred, the orchestra's playing in the lobby."

138

"I'm too tired," he said.

"No. You have to come. They're asking specifically for you."

"Okay." Shuffle, shuffle, shuffle.

When Fred arrived, much to the notice of all assembled, he was escorted to a chair placed right beside the orchestra on the balcony. Front Row Center Plus. And the orchestra began to play . . . Beethoven. They'd prepared a selection especially for Fred. When they'd completed the piece, the director announced that the orchestra was working on several more Beethoven pieces, and they would be making a CD of that work for Fred.

Fred said he was going to have to get a bigger hat to fit his big head.

If nothing else touches your heart this Christmas, that story ought to get you through. I have tears in my eyes just typing it.

This Week in Fred IV
The Gift of Speculation

I'll get right to the bottom line: Fred's getting' a little crazier.

Happy....yes.

Well fed.....yes.

Crazier....as they say in coach-speak, on both sides of the ball.

To wit:
One of the staff had taken a few photos of Fred's constant dinner companions: Little Ralph, Eldon, and the much despised Jacquie . . . much despised by the other biddies for her youthful looks and for her disdain of the accepted order of things, i.e. women sit with other women. In a couple photos, she is leaning into Fred, holding his hand, pearly whites agleam. Nice photos. Happy old folks.

This week the photos were shredded on Fred's coffee table.

"What happened to the pictures, Fred?"

"I didn't want to answer to anybody! A woman scorned, you know."

By now I have learned that pursuing an explanation of such a comment was an invitation into Fred's state of mind. It took a few days and a few attempts for Fred to connect words to his thoughts, but finally it was clear: he's married to Denise and he doesn't want to incur her wrath. It's a delusion that limits his interaction with the present, but one that keeps him contented in his isolation, not a bad delusion. Mild but useful crazy.

Slightly more ominous crazy this: On Friday Dana the head nurse said, "Got one for you." That's always a portent of a story for the book.

"It's been slow lately," says I. "I'm ready for some new material."

By now several of the staff have crowded in, anxious to share in the revelation.

She went right for the jugular, no sugar coating. "Fred shit in an envelope."

"Was it addressed to anyone?" I asked, thinking there might be a Freudian underpinning.

The staff joined the conversation. The nurse who had discovered the, the, the envelope expanded on the details of the discovery, "I knew when I entered the room that something was wrong. Then I saw it. The envelope was sitting on his coffee table."

These guys are unflappable. "Why'd you shit in the envelope, Fred?"

"I thought I was supposed to," his matter-of-fact reply.

Now a guy could leave it at that. Simple enough explanation. But where's the fun in that. So that brings us the title of this week's episode . . . The Gift of Speculation.

So many ways to approach the subject.

Start with "how?" Try to imagine Fred accomplishing such a task. I mean, picture it. It apparently was a very neat job, if you're willing to limit the meaning of "neat."

Then you move on to "why." Was it the nearest receptacle in a moment of extreme need? Did he think he needed a sample for a medical test? Is there actually such a thing as a "shit list," and was Fred mailing off a grievance? Did he imagine he needed to begin assembling personal relics for his imminent sainthood?

And then there's "What's next?" I don't want to go there. We're just going to turn up Fred's meds one notch in hopes of extending his social correctness to the point that he can at least stay at The Home.

The great part about the speculation thing. You guys all get to play.

So, what do you think?

Fred

I knew that Northridge would be the last stop of my journey on Earth. I was tired. I was more than that...I was worn down. I kept drifting in and out. Sometimes I would  be sitting at the dinner table with Margaret, Jan and Stephen. We'd be working on a crossword puzzle, and my mind would latch onto some long forgotten tidbit I had stored somewhere in my brain. I'd shout out the answer to the amazement of the others who had begun to take me for a dullard at this sport. Other times I couldn't hear the clues, or couldn't understand their meaning, or worst of all, I'd know the answer but couldn't find the words before Margaret would proudly snap out the correct solution. I liked it a lot better when the crossword was finished and Stephen would put The Three Tenors on the TV and we could just sit and listen. My spirits could still soar on the magic of their voices.

I lived more on the inside than on the outside. The outside was more of an interruption or a distraction. On the inside I would visit with Ruth. We'd remember the times we'd shared, and we'd make plans to reunite as soon as I could shake the bonds of earth. She would always be wearing that lovely long white gown that she'd wear to formal events.

On the inside Fr. Siro would come to visit me often. He'd remind me of the work yet to be done, of the prayers that still needed uttering, the blessings shared, of the kindnesses to be shown. He urged me on toward my promised sainthood.

I might have been confused about one thing he told me. I know that he'd promised to put my name into his will, and that a large sum, I remember $650,000, would be willed to me to carry out our work. I asked Stephen to check on where the money was, but he was unable to locate any sign of it. I think maybe 'something is rotten in Denmark' on that, but I don't know what else to do about it. I'm awaiting instructions from Fr. Siro.

On the outside, when I had to be on the outside, I liked my home in Northridge. It was as nice a quarters as I could imagine. The staff loved me, and I loved them. My friend, Gregorio, would look in on me every day to see if I needed anything. The women who took care of me were true saints. I had friends in the hallways and friends at the dinner table.

There were two things about Northridge that made it a perfect sanctuary for a crashing senior citizen. I had unrestricted access to an ice cream machine, which was as close to heaven as I was going to get on Earth. And I was free to be me again. I didn't have to try to keep Denise happy, and I could focus on prayer and daily devotions.

Jan and Stephen made sure I got the medical attention I needed. I made it clear to them that I was ready to go, so that in case of a medical emergency, I wanted no extraordinary means to keep me alive. "Just let me go in peace," I instructed them. One day they were going over medical directives with Margaret and me, writing down our instructions. They asked us the question the way it was worded on the form. The question was, "If your heart stops, do you want to be revived?"

I was clear. Absolutely not.

Margaret shreiked, "I want to live!" To which I couldn't help interjecting:

"You want someone to pound on your chest and crush every one of your ribs?" She hadn't thought of it in those terms, and now her medical directives read, "Do Not Resuscitate." Smart move, Big Sister.

Getting to spend my waning days in her company was an unexpected bonus in life. Except for a few years we'd spent our lives apart, me here, her there. Now at the end our paths crossed again. We'd spend time together at Jan and Stephen's, many times sitting quietly side by side, not talking, just listening to Pavarotti.

We would both swoon at the music. When the DVD was finished, we'd just ask to have it start over. I loved those times. A few more days on Earth was a small price to pay for moments like that.

There were a few adventures at what Stephen called "The Home." One night at dinner I was attacked by that crazy woman who lives across the hall from me. She grabbed my hair from behind and started shaking my head. I'll never know what that was about. They kicked her out for that outburst. Good riddance, I say. Not very saintly of me, but a man has his limits, even a saint.

The high school orchestra came to play one day. I tripped on my way into the room and made a spectacle of myself. I hurt my hand when I fell, but I didn't want to miss their performance so I stayed until the end. Then I went to the hospital and had my broken finger splinted. A few weeks later they came back and I was the guest of honor, seated right alongside the orchestra. They had learned to play a Beethoven piece especially for me. Special again, one more time.

Mostly it was quiet there. Just the way I wanted it.

Steve

The Good Samaritan Hospital emergency vehicle, known affectionately to the local coffee shop crowd as "The Unit," pulled out of the Northridge Retirement Center parking lot and headed south to the hospital. The thawed and refrozen ice in the street's gutter crunched under its tires, crackling testimony to Nebraska's fickle November weather, one moment baking, the next freezing. The Unit's siren was still . . . no emergency this.

I walked down the long hallway, past the doors of Little Ralph's apartment, past Minnie's, past Eldon's and Jacquie's, all now closed in the pre-breakfast hours of the community. The Unit had come in silent, and absent any hint of alarm, the residents were stirring toward their ritual morning reunion at the breakfast table. Fred's seat would be empty this morning, and they'd wonder if someone should give him a call. It was not like Fred to miss a meal.

The aides at the nurses' station were anxious for a report.

"How's Freddie?" the young red-haired aide asked. Ashley had a hard time waking Fred for his morning ablution. She loved that word since the day that Fred, the Latin teacher, had introduced it to her. Everyone else at The Home got a bath. Fred got an ablution.

"They're going to check Fred out and hold him for a day, maybe two. His congestive heart condition is getting worse. That's why he was hard to rouse this morning."

"Is he going to be alright?" she asked. Her definition of alright meant Fred shuffling down the hall toward ice cream before breakfast, greeting everyone he passed, singing "Gregorio, Gregorio" to his friend Gregory, or "Gloria in excelsis Deo" in his best church deacon voice. Fred's singing habit had been met at first with mixed reviews, some residents preferring decorous silence. But Fred's persistence had won over all but the most hardened of hearts, and a song-filled hallway was now an accepted and valued feature of The Home, compliments of Fred.

I knew what the aide wanted to hear.

"Not in the way you are asking. Fred's heart is too weak to support him much longer. His doctor says she's surprised that he's still able to function as well as he does."

Tears welled up in her eyes. "Can't they do something to make him better?"

"I know this is going to sound, I don't know what, cruel? hard-hearted? But we need to try to be responsive to what Fred wanted, and he wants to die. I know that's the opposite of the role you've committed yourself to, the care that you give him every day. But Fred goes back to his room after every meal and prays that he be allowed to go to heaven. He wants to meet his God. He wants to catch up with the love of his life, his wife Ruth who preceded him in death years ago. He wants to join his mama and his papa, his sister and brothers, his best pal, Peetie the Praying Dog That Saved San Jose. Fred's convinced that he's a saint. His friend and pastor Father Siro told him so. And Fred said it himself, 'I have to die first before it becomes official.' So Fred's definition of 'better' is to be freed from this body that is failing him and to be allowed to go home."

That argument was no match for the aide's heart. "Do you think he'll live until Christmas?"

"He might. You feed him so well around here that he's put on enough winter fat to get him through till spring thaw."

"But he might not?"

"He might not."

I left to follow Fred to the hospital. Jan was at the hospital and reported via cell phone that she was in the ER and ready to escort Fred to his room. The aide gathered her associates and began hatching a plan.

The Plan

By noon I had returned to The Home and delivered a much anticipated Fred medical update. Several of the staff had gathered at the nurses' station to hear the report. The news wasn't encouraging. His condition was stabilized, and he'd be released to come back tomorrow, but since Fred was adamant about not wanting treatment to extend his lease on his failing body, the likelihood was that another heart event might be his last. Shoulders sagged at the news, unwelcome as it was expected.

"We have a plan we want to discuss with you," Dana said. Heads nodded in agreement.

"Sounds conspiratorial. Spin it out."

"We're afraid Fred might not make it to Christmas. We don't want him to miss it, so we want to have Christmas early for him. A party. Lots of ice cream. All his friends. Would that be okay with you?"

"You folks continue to amaze me. I'm going to be forced to renounce my cynicism about human nature. You're just too caring and kind to let such a notion survive. I think that would be a wonderful plan. Can I horn in on the action?"

"You bet," Dana replied. "Horn away."

"I don't know how many of you know Fred's life story, but I know of at least three Christmases that Fred didn't make it home. The first was in

1917. Fred's father died on Christmas Eve when Fred was just ten months old. His father had emigrated from the mountains of southern Italy early in that century, and by 1917 he was a sometimes prosperous ice cream merchant in Wilmington, North Carolina. I have to believe that was a bleak Christmas in the Stefano household. Mama could speak only broken English, and she was faced with the task of raising seven children on her own. One of the neighbors took Fred to her home to try to help out Rosa Stefano, so Fred wasn't at home for his first Christmas."

"Fred never talked about that," Staci said.

"I doubt Fred remembered that first one. Mag told me that story. But he did remember the next one. His mama tried to keep the family together but the burden was too heavy. Times were tough back then, and she couldn't make and sell enough candy to support that brood. The Catholic priest at St. Mary's parish stepped in and arranged for several of the children to be sent off to orphanages in the North Carolina countryside. Margaret was sent to Belmont Abbey. Fred was sent to a place called Nazareth. Think of the irony of that . . . Nazareth, the childhood home of Jesus, and of Fred. Maybe that connection was why Fred was drawn back to the church late in his life. In any case, late in 1929, when Fred was twelve years old, the stock market crashed and money was scarce. There wasn't enough money in the poor box to afford Fred a bus ticket to Wilmington, so he spent that Christmas alone in Nazareth, wishing that he could be with his family. He could describe that room in intimate detail, the stone floor, the crucifix on the wall above the thin cot, the cold mountain air falling in through the single-paned window. Fred remembered that Christmas."

"That's so sad," said Nesha. I noticed a tear or two in the eyes of several of the staff. Maybe a few in mine too.

"He remembered another lost Christmas. It was 1944. Fred was in the Army Air Corp, stationed in Bari, a small town on the southeast coast of Italy. Fred's squadron had the mission of flying reconnaissance to spot weather and guide Allied bombers to Axis targets in Germany,

149

Austria and Eastern Europe. The Allies were trying to push their way up through Italy to attack Germany's southern flank. No one knew at that time who would win that war, but Fred knew for sure that he was cold, wet, scared, and a long way from home. It's an interesting coincidence that he wasn't many miles from Casal Cassinese, the small mountain village near Monte Cassino that had been his family's home in Italy. So here was Fred, once again, unable to make it home for Christmas."

If there had been a dry eye before that story, there were none left now.

"So what I'm thinking is that maybe we can make this the year that Fred catches up on all his lost Christmases. This is his home now. He's been happier here than at any time since his wife passed away fifteen years ago. You folks have made it so."

"It wouldn't be hard to do," Courtney said. "All Fred needs for a party is a bowl of ice cream. Let's just chip in, buy every kind of ice cream we can find, and have a Freddie Christmas four days running. That way we can catch up on the three that he missed, and celebrate this year's early so he'll be sure not to miss it."

That motion was seconded and adopted by a round of quiet applause. Phyllis was deputized to collect the money, buy the ice cream and secret it in the kitchen's freezers. Brenda said she'd arrange for fresh cookies, hot out of the oven each day. Pam volunteered to organize the party room and invite the residents. I volunteered to tell a short story each day, relating details of the past Christmas that Fred had missed, confident that Fred's friends and neighbors could all tell such stories of their own. The concept of the party was expanded to include the sharing of these memories. The plan was launched.

The Parties

Fred and I arrived back at The Home without fanfare the next morning. I had intended to ensconce Fred on his couch, insert an Andre Rieu (I finally remembered his name) disc into the DVD player,

150

and leave Fred in his earthly version of heaven. Ashley and Staci met us at the door, commandeered Fred's wheelchair, and announced that they'd take it from there.

"We got you some flowers, Fred, and a box of chocolates," was the last I heard as they pushed Fred own the hallway. Little Ralph's door was open, and when he saw the procession pass by, he fell in behind to welcome his friend home.

"How are you feeling, Freddie?" Staci asked.

"Fine. I'm fine," was Fred's characteristic answer. Neither of the aides could ever remember any other answer. No matter the situation, Fred was always "fine." Maybe it was this sunny disposition that endeared him to his caregivers. He was grateful for the smallest of attention, and never failed express his gratitude.

"You going to be ready for some lunch in a little bit?" Ashley asked.

"I'm a little tired right now," Fred replied. "I'd like to take a nap. Maybe you could stop in later and put on the TV for me, the Rieu one with the pastoral scenes."

They both knew Fred's inventory of classical DVDs . "I'll do that for you," Ashley offered.

"Thank you."

Day two of Fred's return was Day One of Fred's Make-up Christmases. At 2 in the afternoon, Courtney invited Fred to join her for a bowl of ice cream, an invitation he couldn't refuse. When they walked into the Ridge Room, Fred was surprised to see a number of fellow ice cream eaters. And by the Christmas tree in the center of the room.

"Is it Christmas again already?" he asked.

"It's a make-up Christmas," Pam announced.

"Make up for what?" Fred asked.

"For Christmases you missed," she replied.

"What do you mean?" Fred asked.

"Your sister Margaret will tell that story," Pam said, yielding the floor to the white-haired big sister, "big" being an age-relative term for a 4 foot 10, 90 pound old lady.

"Fred," she began, "you were too little to remember your first Christmas, but Papa had died the day before and it was a madhouse at 611 Castle Street that day. Mary Barbieri was Mama's best friend, and she took you over to her house to rescue you from all the confusion, so you spent your first Christmas Day away from your home. The staff and all your friends here decided that they'd make up for that lost Christmas today."

"That is very nice," Fred said. "Thank you."

"Is there anything else you'd like to say?' Margaret asked.

"No. I don't think so," Fred replied. "Courtney said there'd be ice cream."

So ice cream there was. For all assembled. And then a rousing version of "Silent Night" led by Fred's loud and deeply-timbered church voice.

Fred was a little more suspicious the next day when Sam invited him out for an afternoon dish of ice cream. But ice cream is ice cream.

The crowd in the Ridge Room had doubled from the day before, word having spread through the hallways by the previous day's attendees that a special event was happening. Fred was again wheeled into the room, past the tree, to the head table. Little Ralph, Jacquie and Eldon were already seated there to greet him.

"Is it dinnertime already?" Fred asked as he was deposited next to his daily tablemates.

"No Fred," Jacquie replied. "It's a catch-up Christmas day for you. Remember how you told us at lunch one day about your first Christmas at the orphanage?"

"I don't remember telling you about it, but I remember it clear as day."

"I think folks here would like to hear that story too," Jacquie encouraged.

Fred launched into a description of his Nazareth Christmas. He described the early-morning mass in the classic old stone chapel; the glorious voices of the seminarians who had come to Nazareth to sing their Gregorian chant that morning; the floral arrangements that surrounded the crèche in front of the altar. Greg, standing in the back of the room, couldn't miss the reference to the chant, surmising correctly that it was the inspiration for Fred's hallway hallelujahs. If anyone had been expecting a note of sadness or resentment at Fred's being alone on that day, they were disappointed. Fred remembered only the glory of it all.

"Did you miss your family?" Pam asked.

"Oh sure," Fred replied. "I wanted to be home with all of them, but I couldn't be, so I made the best of where I was. The priest let me serve mass that day, so I got an important job. I liked that a lot."

When it was clear to Pam, the mistress of ceremonies, that Fred had completed his story, she invited others in the room to share any story they might have about Christmases where they hadn't been able to make it home. No one stepped forward at first, but then in the back of the room, Jennie rose from her chair and spoke haltingly in a stroke-impaired voice that was audible only to those very close to her.

"I remember once we couldn't get home. A snowstorm caught us in the wagon halfway between home and town. The Gerlachs took us in and we spent two days sitting around the stove playing cards and telling stories, and two nights sleeping on their floor. It was one of the best Christmases ever." Then she sat back down.

The audience nodded in understanding. Many had experienced Nebraska storms, and many had been stranded to the mercy of neighbors and strangers. When no one volunteered another story, Fred spoke up. "So when's the ice cream?"

On the third day of Fred's Make-up Christmas, the Ridge Room was full. Neither residents nor staff wanted to miss the party. Fred was especially tired that afternoon, and even the promise of ice cream took second money to the concept of a nap. It took Courtney several tries to convince Fred that his presence was important to a roomful of friends that wanted to hear the story of Fred's Christmas in Bari, Italy. Fred finally acceded to her pleadings and she helped Fred onto the seat of his walker which doubled as a makeshift wheel chair. She had shuttled him down the hallway to the nurses' station when Fred remembered something.

"We need to go back to my room," he ordered.

"No deal," Courtney replied. "We're heading for an ice cream party."

"No," Fred countered, "we have to get it."

"What do we have to get?" she asked.

Fred couldn't put the word to the thought and struggled to express himself. "You know, the, uh, that thing..." Courtney could see that Fred was getting agitated. "Let's head back there," she said. "You can show me what we have to get."

Fred relaxed at the offer, and it took him only moments to retrieve what he was after, an aging book that showed signs of fifty years of wear. It was "The Story of a Squadron," the diary of his years in World War II. "

"This will help me remember that Christmas," he said.

"You're really getting into the spirit of this thing," she encouraged. "Let's go tell them a real story."

"I need you to read it for me," Fred said.

"The folks want to hear you tell the story, Fred," Courtney countered.

"I'm too tired," Fred replied. "I'll try to tell them a little bit about what was going on over there at that time, but sometimes I just can't find the words to say what I'm thinking. If I get stuck like that, I want you to read them the paragraph for the date Dec. 25, 1944."

"No worries, Fred, I'll be right there for you."

The room was full when Fred was wheeled to the table at the front of the room. It was decorated with a Christmas wreath, bright red candles, and plates of goodies baked by the ladies of The Home. Many had been first-rate cooks in their own farmhouse kitchens and delighted in bringing their own Christmas favorite treats to this special party.

Fred looked over the array of delectables with the eye of a depression-era child, imagining how each would taste and wondering where the leftovers might be headed.

Pam opened the ceremonies by leading the partiers in a rousing rendition of "Hark the Herald Angels Sing." Fred's voice, usually the loudest at The Home's sing-along sessions, was unusually muted. When Pam mentioned the change, Fred said, "I'm just tired."

Then Pam asked Fred to tell the story of his Third Missed Christmas. Fred said he'd try.

"Actually, it was the third Christmas that we had been away from home. We'd been in England, in Morocco, in Algeria, in Tunisia running the Germans out of North Africa for two years. When we finally got that done, we shipped across the Mediterranean to Naples and then across the mountains to Bari."

Fred's memory and his voice seemed to be ten years younger as he recounted the tale.

"At the end of 1944, we were trying to push our way up through Italy to attack the Germans from the south. Our mission was mostly to provide weather and reconnaissance information for Allied bombers. We flew over targets in Italy, Germany, Romania, Austria, the whole of Eastern Europe."

The clarity of Fred's memory surprised everyone in the hall. They were all accustomed to Fred's difficulty in matching words to thoughts, and this day things were different. It was like the barrier between his brain and his speech had been erased.

"The reports coming from headquarters, and from German radio broadcasts for that matter, were alarming. The Germans had launched a major offensive, penetrating deep behind our lines into Belgium, and it appeared they might be on their way to capturing Paris. So on Christmas Day that year, we knew we had a job to do, and that was keep our planes flying over enemy targets. Breakfast that day was the usual, SOS." That reference brought a laugh from the other veterans.

"We got our P-38s and A-20s into the air, over the targets, and back safely by noon. Then the mood changed. The officers took over our everyday jobs, on the line, in camp, and in Bari, and we knew we had a few hours to enjoy Christmas day. That evening the officers served us a turkey dinner with all the trimmings. It was the best meal we'd had in months. The mood in camp that night was . . ." Fred struggled for

156

the word. He finally found it . . . . "'miraculous.' For a few hours we forgot about the war as we sang songs and told stories late into the night. One by one we drifted off to our beds to a short, cold night's sleep. The next morning we were back on the line well before dawn, launching our planes on their way north. Christmas was now 365 days off in the future. We all wondered if we'd be home by next Christmas."

Fred leaned back in his chair. He was exhausted by telling of the story of his Italian missed Christmas. Courtney, who had stayed by his side, said, "Fred, I haven't heard you say that much in the months that you've been here."

"I was on autopilot," Fred smiled. "Now it's time for a landing."

Floyd took over. "I remember where I was that Christmas." He told that story. Then Eldon. Then Little Ralph. Then Big Ralph. Memories flooded the room, and more than a few hankies were retrieved from pocket or purse to dab wet eyes and cheeks. Fred didn't hear those stories. His head slumped as he drifted into a sitting sleep.

Fred didn't make the early Christmas party the next day. During that night Fred suffered a stroke in his sleep, the sleep he'd started in his chair listening to Floyd's story. He'd been taken to the hospital in a coma. The staff decided that they'd have the party, if not as an early Christmas for Fred, then in his honor. The room was again full, the tables again piled with home baked delicacies. This time, without prompting from the staff, Doris asked if she could tell about the time she was in a USO company that hosted a tent full of troops for a Christmas dinner in North Platte. Then Minnie, in her timid voice, remembered a lonely Christmas stranded in a snowbound train station. Pam, ever the watchful guardian angel, could tell that many were having trouble hearing the stories. She suggested that folks just share their stories around the table where they were sitting. This rearrangement opened the door to a host of storytellers who wouldn't, couldn't, speak before a crowd but who could spin a story to a table-sized audience. One story triggered the next, and an hour later the tales were still being told.

Ruth leaned over to the little Big Sister who had quietly attended all the make-up Christmas parties.

"Fred's not going to make it, is he?" she shared the expectation of all in The Home.

"No," Margaret said. "I don't think he'll recover this time."

"It's a shame Fred can't be here to see this. His life was sad."

"I don't think Fred ever thought it was sad," Margaret replied. "He got off to such a hard start that he was grateful for everything that came after. He thought living here was like living in a country club. No, Fred was just grateful for everything: every meal, every ice cream cone; every Andre Rieu concert on his DVD; every kindness showed him."

"I still think it's sad that he didn't even make it to the last of his make-up Christmases," Ruth said. "He wasn't at home for his first Christmas, for the Christmas spent in the cold room at the orphanage, for the years he was overseas fighting in the war. And now he missed his last make-up Christmas."

"Ruth," Margaret said, "Fred might not have been at home for those Christmases, but he's on his way home now. The little boy from the orphanage in Nazareth is going home to join his more famous friend from Nazareth. It's what he prayed for everyday, and now he's finally on his way."

Fred

There's a lot of activity going on around me now, and all I can do is sit inside this still body and watch.

Sometimes my mind is as clear as a Carolina morning, dry air falling in from the west. Sometimes now it's like the days when the fog would settle in over Silver Lake and you couldn't see the end of the dock.

I know one thing as sure as I know anything, which is a tenuous concept these days. I know that I am a lucky man.

I'm old now. From the outside I know I look dimmed. And I am. But not all the time. Sometimes I can see and hear and remember. And I just stay inside my wizened body and take it all in. I'm grateful to be surrounded by people who love the shrunken me. Thank you, family. I love you all. I'll be going home soon.

Jan

I got to the PCU room before Fred arrived. It was clear from his chart that he'd had a massive stroke and was unlikely to reawaken. I called Radiology to confirm the results.

"It would take a miracle for him to regain consciousness," was the report.

"I think we've already gotten our miracle. Thanks." I'm not sure the radiologist understood that comment.

Way to go, Fred. Your prayers have been answered. You're on your way.

Fred was wheeled in shortly, breathing comfortably but with no signs of consciousness. The nurse and an aid transferred Fred to the PCU bed, and asked if Fred had a medical directive.

"He does. He's slipped into a peaceful sleep and he doesn't want any efforts made to revive him. It is in his charts."

"What about IV fluids? We can at least keep him hydrated," she offered.

"If he appears to be in pain, I'd like you to give him something to alleviate that. But nothing else. I've had many conversations with Fred and he was very clear on his wishes...no intervention to keep him alive." She understood.

"Sometimes a patient can hear what's going on around him even if he doesn't appear to be awake. Does he have a favorite TV channel?"

"He does. Let's put The Animal Channel on. He watches that all the time."

The nurse tuned the overhead television to that channel, then had one further question for me. "In case he does wake up, what would he like best to eat?" Another kind consideration.

"Ice cream," I told her. "He loves ice cream."

From behind me came, "Ice cream. That's my favorite."

Those were Fred's last words. He never woke again.
I thought it was a perfect ending.

Steve

My brothers and I were able to do Fred one last 'solid.' We owed him more than that.

Fred's last wishes included this: "I want my ashes scattered in the Pacific Ocean, so that I can join my beloved wife Ruth."

Each year Michael, Mark, Julie and I, joined by the rest of our family, get together for 'The JB,' a gathering in memory and celebration of the life of our departed brother John. That year's event was to be hosted by Mark in Petaluma, a short drive to the Pacific. We dutifully loaded Fred's ashes into the golf cart and carried him 18 holes while we dueled it out for the coveted JB Trophy.

The round concluded and the victor determined, we made our way to the secluded beach off the eighteenth green of Bodega Harbour Golf Links. Each of us who had known him spoke a few words, mostly memories of one of Fred's antics. Those second generation attendees who had not known him were introduced to an important part of their heritage.

Memories shared and tears shed, we waded into the surf and slipped the cover from the canister containing Fred. Actually Fred's ashes. Nothing ever contained Fred. Mark poured the ashes into the retreating surf and he floated free. He joined Ruth. We joined Fred. We did a reset on our embrace of Fred, removing the label 'Eccentric' from our memory of him, and replacing it with one that read 'Essential.'

'Big' Sister got a chance to say,

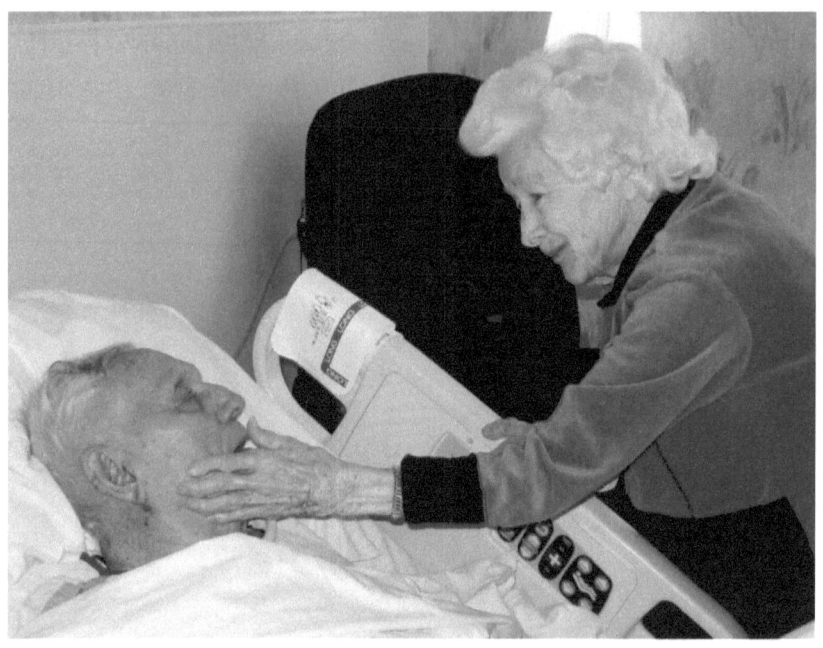

"Goodbye little brother. Don't forget me when you get to heaven."

Family Soil

At first it was a small seed, welcomed into a bed of family soil.
It needed a place to rest, a place we could well afford to offer.
It drew little of our store, rested, snuggled, gained purchase in its new place.
It sent out tentative roots, gratefully accepting this nourishing spot.

It was only weeks before the first shoots broke free into sunlight,
And a few more days before the first buds appeared.
      Then another,
            And another,
                  And then scores more.

Flowers of joy, petals of smiles
      And sighs,
            And peaceful rest.

Flowers of appreciation, thanks, prayer, and spoken blessings.

Flowers of the comfort of safety and security.

Flowers of stories, At first hazy
But always growing as details were remembered and accumulated.

Stories from before memory.

Stories created to fill holes that no memory held.

Stories of the tastes of Papa's sweet ice cream, and of his voice as he sold it on the street corner.

Stories of the orphanage, and the nuns' sweet care,
      Of the prayers, and the masses, the litanies and the rosaries,
            And of the stone floors bearing praying knees.

Then stories of the war
Shelters holding crouching soldiers, more curious than afraid.

Sergeant's orders comically acknowledged and then ignored.
> "He told me to go down in the basement and stand
> guard over that Jerry's un-exploded bomb. Hell, that
> wasn't my specialty."

Then stories of peace
    And love
        And marriage
           And death
              And loss
                And loneliness . . . no,
                    not loneliness
It was gratefulness at the memory of love.

And now it's a blur of memory and fantasy.
"Was it real? Was it a dream? It seemed so real."

Stay in the family soil, Uncle. It doesn't matter if it's real or not.

It's all the same.

You are safe here.

www.ingramcontent.com/pod-product-compliance
Lightning Source LLC
Chambersburg PA
CBHW061249280526
45784CB00002B/689